THE ULTIMATE GUIDE TO SQUIRREL HUNTING

Everything You Need to Know to Hunt
This Popular Game Animal

BOB GOOCH

The Lyons Press
Guilford, Connecticut
An imprint of The Globe Pequot Press

The Lyons Press is an imprint of The Globe Pequot Press.

Printed in the United States of America

10 9 8 7 6 5 4 3 2 1

ISBN 1-59228-587-2

Library of Congress Cataloging-in-Publication Data is available on file.

CONTENTS

ACKNOWLEDGMENTS

I am deeply grateful for the unselfish attitudes of the many people who helped me gather the material for this book. Their common interest in the tree squirrels and the important role they play in the traditional sport of hunting and our environment was demonstrated by the eagerness with which they responded to my requests for information.

Dedicated professional managers of fish and game departments throughout America completed questionnaires, informing me of the status of the squirrel populations in each of the fifty states, and passed on a wealth of general knowledge. (The information they provided concerning their respective states is condensed in chapter five, and this same data appeared under my byline in capsule form in *Field & Stream* magazine.) The frank replies from the few states in which squirrels are not hunted were also helpful in establishing the natural range of the various squirrels and the local popularity of squirrel hunting.

Particularly valuable were research papers from the game departments of the states of Arizona, California, Colorado, Delaware, Florida, Illinois, Indiana, Kentucky, Louisiana, Maine, Michigan, Minnesota, Mississippi, Missouri, Nebraska, New Hampshire, New Jersey, New Mexico, New York, North Carolina, Ohio, Oregon, Pennsylvania, Rhode Island, Tennessee, Texas, Virginia, and West Virginia. Much of the information contained in the chapter on the management of tree squirrels came from these excellent reports. Missouri, in particular, has done an amazing amount of research on the several species of squirrels available in that top squirrel-hunting state.

Fellow outdoor writers Walton Lowry of Alabama, John Heuston of Arkansas, Judd Cooney of Colorado, Charley Waterman of Florida, Bert Biehl of Hawaii, Elmer Keith of Idaho, Don Carpenter of Maryland, Jack Mell of Michigan, Jack Connor of Minnesota, Dudley B. Heiliger of Mississippi, B. B. Watson of Missouri, Bill Browning of Montana, Woody Price of North Carolina, Dick Paugh of Ohio, Pete Gardner of Rhode Island, Herb Johnson of South Carolina, Carlos Vinson of Tennessee, Percy Angwin of Vermont, Fred Peterson of Washington, and Jack Richard of Wyoming passed on to me much valuable information on the status of squirrels in their home territories. Bert Biehl confirmed the absence of squirrels in Hawaii, an island state otherwise rich in a great variety of game animals. Several of these fine outdoorsmen and writers have passed on, leaving a rich legacy of outdoor journalism we can still enjoy.

Over half a century of hunting has brought me in contact with many fine sportsmen. We have hunted together, shared campfires, and swapped tales and hunting tips. The practical side of hunting is developed in this manner, and I am sure my friends will not object to my passing on what I can to readers in this book.

Finally, I am indebted to my wife, Ginny, and two daughters, Pam and Pat. At most they have complained only mildly when I stumbled out of the house at an early hour for a dawn rendezvous with the bushytail population in a nearby hickory grove. I am also indebted to Jay Cassell, editorial director at The Lyons Press, and his assistant, Christine Duffy, whose editorial advice and encouragement has been invaluable as I put in many long hours writing the manuscript.

INTRODUCTION

My first game was an English sparrow—a pesky little import bagged with a BB gun. I recall very vividly dropping my first quail, and I believe the persistent memory of a bouncing cottontail tumbling head over heels at the crack of the family Long Tom is the recollection of my first rabbit. There was a lot of small game in my budding hunting career, but those firsts stand out and linger on. And what hunter could forget his first deer or turkey? But they came later, with a lot of other big game.

Between the sparrows, the rabbits, and the quail came countless gray squirrels. Oddly, though, my first squirrel is lost in the haze of the passing years, a mist such as that which often clothed the early morning sunbeams slanting through the tall timber of my favorite squirrel woods.

One of my father's hunting companions, and a frequent visitor to our farm, presented my brother and me with BB guns. At an early age we learned the rudiments of hunting and shooting. But we were graduated directly from those little rifles to booming 12-gauge shotguns, a move not unlike jumping from little league football to the Green Bay Packers. Money was scarce back in those days of the Great Depression, and it was either move to the big guns and accept their mule-like kick or stay with the little BB guns. We learned to grit our teeth—probably closing our eyes—and hang on as we pulled the trigger. But as a fat bushytail usually came tumbling out of a tall oak or hickory, the punishing jolt was soon forgotten.

There were many more squirrels than quail and rabbits in my boyhood hunting days, and I suspect that is the reason the memory of that first bushytail escapes me. I spent many happy hours in the squirrel woods, and I still enjoy squirrel hunting just as much, these many seasons later. Evidently, so do thousands of other small-game hunters, because the squirrel is generally considered one of the most popular game animals in America.

When I finally earned enough money for a single-shot .22-caliber rifle I learned the true joy of squirrel hunting. That inexpensive rifle was equipped with the crudest of open sights, but with it I was able to attain reasonable accuracy. However, bagging a squirrel required close shooting, and I realized I'd found a greater challenge than ever before—one I had not experienced previously with that old shotgun.

I still consider the little .22-caliber rifle the ideal firearm for squirrel hunting; today, I rarely hunt squirrels with a shotgun. But of course my present squirrel rifles are fitted with low-powered telescopic sights, a tremendous improvement over the old open sights.

A few years ago I developed an interest in bowhunting and now I take another exciting new challenge into the hickory groves—hunting squirrels with archery tackle. Many states hold early archery seasons during which squirrels are legal along with other game. Deer are the target of most bowhunters, but squirrels offer far more shooting opportunities. They are my favorite quarry with bow and arrow.

Perhaps that is the reason why squirrels enjoy such a lofty position among our nation's game animals. Everyone hunts them—the sharpshooting rifleman, the smooth-swinging shotgunner, the dedicated bowhunter, and even devotees of the smokepole, or muzzleloader.

Every state except tropical Hawaii boasts a huntable population of tree squirrels, but their popularity varies tremendously. They are completely protected in a few western states, where interest in squirrel hunting is the lowest. Generally, though, the seasons are long, the game abundant, and the bag limits liberal. What more could a small-game hunter ask for?

Much of the credit for the popularity tree squirrels have among hunters must go to the frisky little gray squirrel, the true bushytail. An inhabitant of dense hardwood forests, the gray is an extremely adaptable little animal, and he can make himself just as much at home in a city park as in the deep woods. Suburban yards, farm woodlots, extensive forests—all are acceptable to the gray squirrel. Thanks to the gray, squirrel hunting is seldom out of reach for most Americans.

No matter what your weapon of choice, you can usually partake in the inexpensive sport of squirrel hunting relatively close to home—something all hunters can appreciate after chasing big game on expensive hunts across the continent. The squirrel appeals to everyone from barefoot country boys to serious lifelong nimrods.

Chapter
1

MEET THE SQUIRRELS

High in the treetops of America many species of squirrel provide immeasurable hours of hunting pleasure for some of this country's finest sportsmen. For a number of years, the squirrel was generally regarded as the number-two game animal in America, second only to the popular cottontail rabbit. This may or may not hold true today, but certainly it remains one of our most sought after game animals. Game managers may someday reduce the joy of squirrel hunting to cold figures—hunter hours and days—but even then it will be impossible to measure the real recreational value this plucky little game animal has afforded hunters since the dawn of the New World.

Early settlers discovered an abundance of squirrels in the mast-rich hardwood forests of the new continent, and the frisky little rodents soon won the respect of the hardy pioneers. While these highly practical men and women hunted primarily for the table, good clean fun soon became an important by-product of squirrel hunting. And the squirrel's popularity didn't diminish as the pioneers pushed westward across a game-filled land. In fact, the demand for a good squirrel gun brought forth the famous Kentucky Rifle, an extremely accurate muzzleloading rifle

Three generations of squirrel hunters: grandson Ben Hallissy flanked by his father, Jim Hallissy, and his grandfather, author Bob Gooch.

capable of putting a ball through the tiny head of a gray squirrel at fifty yards.

While the squirrel family includes a wide range of species— ground squirrels, mantle squirrels, antelope squirrels, flying squirrels, and even chipmunks, prairie dogs, and woodchucks, to name a few—it is the tree squirrels that we are concerned with here. With only a few exceptions, tree squirrels are officially recognized as game animals throughout most of the United States, a distinction none of the other squirrels can claim, though some of them, such as prairie dogs and woodchucks, receive a good deal of attention from varmint hunters.

Large bushy tails, small round heads, and sharp protruding teeth are common physical characteristics of the tree squirrels, which are classified as rodents. They bark and chatter when disturbed and possess an amazing ability to fade into their surround-

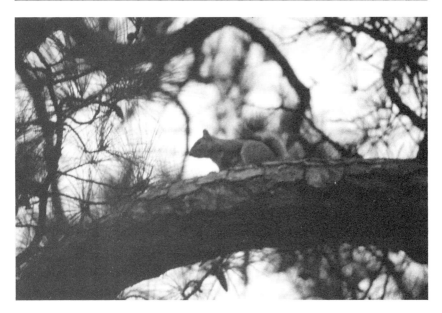

Squirrels are uniquely designed for life in the treetops.

ings. Even in the dead of winter, when trees are bare of foliage, a cagey squirrel can flatten itself against the gray trunk of a tall oak and become almost impossible to detect. Squirrels are agile and alert and capable of moving rapidly through the treetops, leaping expertly from one swaying branch to another. The busy tail serves as a rudder, stabilizing the squirrel's flight, and as a parachute, cushioning its fall during a leap to the ground from high in a tree.

With the exception of the flying squirrel, all species are diurnal—active mainly during the daylight hours.

The squirrel's habits are fairly predictable, though they vary some from season to season and in periods of foul weather. It is usually up at dawn and headed for breakfast in a favorite nut tree—hickory, pecan, beech, and oak are preferred. If nuts are scarce, a meal may consist of seeds, buds, pinecones, or ripe corn from the field of a hard-working but exasperated farmer. For some reason, squirrels seem to dash from their dens and race away to feed at dawn but take their time at dusk, setting a slow pace as they head back to those dens for the night. A shot at dawn may be hard to come by, but you'll find it much easier at dusk.

In winter the squirrel may scurry around on the ground, digging in the leaves or snow for food, possibly for nuts it stored in late summer or fall. It often feeds until midmorning. Then comes a siesta—back in the den tree or stretched out in the sun high on the limb of a big oak. It usually resumes feeding by late afternoon and then heads leisurely home before darkness falls.

THE EASTERN GRAY SQUIRREL

The eastern gray squirrel, *Sciurus carolinensis*, is the true bushytail. Because of its abundance and wide distribution, the little gray gets the top rating among hunters who follow the sport.

The gray is an extremely adaptable little animal, living in city parks, suburbia, and farm woodlots, though its preferred habitat is the tall timber—dense hardwood forests rich in mast and den trees. It is found in timbered river valleys, along mountain slopes, among the rolling hills, and on the flat coastal plains.

Although the black phase of the eastern gray is fairly common, typical squirrel coloration is a salt-and-pepper gray with a white belly. Both the gray and white parts of the coat are frequently tinged with yellow, tan, or brown. Hunters, misled by the rusty appearance of these off-color grays, sometimes incorrectly refer to them as fox squirrels. In many parts of the South the gray is called the cat squirrel because of its catlike tail.

The average gray weighs approximately a pound to a pound and a half and measures eighteen to twenty inches from the tip of its nose to the tip of its bushy tail. The carefully preened banner tail is approximately nine inches long. A few healthy squirrels live to the ripe old age of fifteen years, but the average life span is

The gray squirrel is heavily hunted in the eastern United States.

much less. Size and lifespan vary considerably from one part of the squirrel's range to another.

The squirrel's chatter is instantly recognizable to experienced woodsmen. Its harsh *quak-quak-quak-a-a-a-a* and scolding *chirr* are always welcome sounds to a hunter moving quietly through the squirrel woods.

In their studies of the gray squirrel, wildlife managers have established several subspecies, although in most states all grays are lumped into the general category of *Sciurus carolinensis.* Alabama biologists list the southern gray squirrel as *S. c. carolinensis*, and the Louisiana gray squirrel is *S. c. fuliginosus.* The Texas Latin name is also *S. c. carolinensis*, which seems to be an attempt to distinguish between the northern gray and the southern gray.

New Jersey and Wisconsin, for example, call their gray squirrel the northern gray, *S. c. leucotis*. In Rhode Island the gray squirrel is known scientifically as *S. c. pennsylvanicus*. In Illinois, a top squirrel-hunting state, reference is made to two subspecies of the gray squirrel: *S. c. pennsylvanicus* in the northern two-thirds of the state and *S. c. carolinensis* elsewhere.

Of course, the average hunter could care less about the various subspecies, and the difference between them would only be evident to a professional biologist. The gray, because of its wide distribution, is the most often pursued tree squirrel, particularly in the southern states where squirrel hunting has been a popular pastime for many generations.

THE WESTERN GRAY SQUIRREL

The western gray squirrel, *Sciurus griseus*, looks much like its eastern cousin, though it is slightly larger. Found only in the Far

The western gray squirrel is found primarily in the Far West. It is protected in some areas and rarely hunted elsewhere.

West, the game potential of this squirrel has never been realized because westerners do not value their squirrel hunting as highly as easterners do. The western gray is native to California, Oregon, and Washington. The coat of the western gray rarely has the rusty tinge so prevalent among the eastern squirrels; in Oregon the gray is commonly known as the silver gray squirrel.

A third gray squirrel, the Arizona gray, is found in Arizona and New Mexico. Scientifically, the Arizona gray is known as *Sciurus arizonensis* in both states. It is regarded as a very shy animal, furtive and secretive in its movements. This squirrel averages approximately two feet from the tip of its nose to the tip of its tail — about the same size as the western gray. Because of its secretive habits the Arizona gray is difficult to hunt and receives very little attention from hunters.

THE ABERT SQUIRREL

The lack of interest in the western and Arizona grays among the ranks of the hunting fraternity does not carry over to the tuft-eared, or Abert, squirrel, which is also found in the Southwest. This animal is usually considered the most handsome of the tree squirrels.

For most Arizona hunters the squirrel-hunting season begins and ends with the season on Aberts (*Sciurus aberti*), the most widespread of the Arizona squirrels. Attractively marked, the Abert is dark gray on its back and white underneath, and this color combination continues to the long bushy tail. It bears a distinctive rust-colored streak down its back and wears a pair of jaunty, long, tufted ears. During the winter months these ears bear tassels reaching an inch or so. In New Mexico the Abert is commonly called the tassel-eared squirrel.

The Abert squirrel is larger than the eastern gray, filling the slot between the eastern and western gray in size. The long bushy

The Abert is an interesting squirrel found mostly in Arizona, New Mexico, and Colorado. (Bob Whitaker)

tail makes up almost half of the Abert's length, and contributes to the animal's graceful appearance. The call of this squirrel resembles the whistle or snort of a startled white-tailed deer. In fact, the squirrel also uses it when startled, evidently as a warning cry. It can be described as a soft *chuff chuff.* The Abert squirrel was a favorite food among early explorers of the Southwest, even in competition with such delicacies as venison, bear meat, turkey, and pigeon.

New Mexico authorities separate their Abert squirrels into a trio of subspecies. In the southwestern corner of the state the Abert is known scientifically as *Sciurus aberti aberti.* Its Latin label in northern New Mexico is *S. a. mimus,* and in the Chuska Mountains biologists call it *S. a. chuscensis.*

There is also a small population of Abert squirrels in Colorado, but they are completely protected.

The closely related Kaibab squirrel, *S. a. kaibabensis,* is found north of the Grand Canyon in the Kaibab National Forest. Its belly is almost completely dark, but the tail is nearly all white. The Kaibab is protected throughout most of its range.

THE FOX SQUIRREL

The fox squirrel, *Sciurus niger,* is the jumbo member of the tree squirrel clan. Although this big squirrel is lazy, deliberate, and awkward in its movements when compared to the agile gray, with which it shares much of its range, the size of the fox squirrel makes it a hunting prize. Many exceed two feet from the tips of their tails to the ends of their noses. Mature specimens can weigh as much as two and a half pounds.

The colors of this squirrel are the most varied of all the tree squirrels, ranging from a yellowish-rust to gray, and in a few instances to almost black. White is not as predominant as it is in the coat of the eastern gray. The fox's coat has a hairy appearance and does not look as well groomed as those of other squirrels.

Because the fox squirrel is much less wary than the gray, its status as a game animal suffers, particularly among hunters who enjoy the challenge of the stalk or the opportunity to outwit a shrewd game animal.

The large fox squirrel is close behind the eastern gray in popularity among hunters. (Texas Parks and Wildlife)

The fox squirrel was probably never as abundant as the gray in much of the common range shared by the two species, and it is not nearly as adaptable to changes in its environment. Lazy by nature, the fox is not a provident harvester like the smaller gray. Consequently, it suffers more from hunger late in the winter. Its approach to survival is to build up a heavy layer of fat rather than to store nuts for the long winters.

In keeping with its languid nature, the fox squirrel avoids early hours and feeds later in the morning than the other squirrels. It feeds again in midafternoon and then retires early. This oversized member of the squirrel family is an inhabitant of the edges of the forests, fencerows and thickets, the borders of cypress swamps, and mixed stands of timber.

Game managers in Wisconsin, Michigan, and Iowa give their fox squirrels the scientific tag *Sciurus niger rufiventer*, and casually refer to them as western fox squirrels. In Illinois they are known as eastern fox squirrels and are scientifically labeled *S. n. linnaeus*. Alabama biologists also refine their fox squirrel classifications into Bachman's fox squirrels, *S. n. bachmani*, and southern fox squirrels, *S. n. niger*.

THE OTHER TREE SQUIRRELS

Of little significance as game animals, but of interest to the many outdoorsmen and women who enjoy viewing all types of wildlife, are the small red or pine squirrels, the chickarees or Douglas squirrels, and the flying squirrels.

The red squirrel, the smallest of the tree squirrels, is an inhabitant of the coniferous forests of our mountain and northern states. It fills the forests with its noisy chatter and is often referred to as the "boomer." Wildlife biologists know it as *Tamiasciurus hudsonicus*, with refinements including *T. h. mogollonensis*, *T. h. fremonti*, *Sciurus hudsonicus*, *T. h. loquax*, and *T. h. minnesota*.

Although not usually considered a game animal, the red squirrel thrives in many western states.

The chickaree is found in the tall pine and spruce forests of the Northwest. Its Latin name is *Tamisaciurus douglasi*, but it is also known as *T. d. albolimbatus* and *Tamiasciurus fremonti*. In appearance and habits the chickaree, or Douglas squirrel, is much like the little red squirrel.

The flying squirrel does not actually fly, but by extending its legs and stretching the loose fold of skin between the front and back legs it is able to glide long distances. There are two sub-species of flying squirrels. The larger northern flying squirrel is called *Glaucomys sabrinus* and the smaller southern species is known scientifically as *Glaucomys volans*. Both enjoy complete protection in most states.

Finally, in arid Arizona—home of the Abert and Kaibab squirrels, the Arizona gray and the saucy little red squirrel—there is still another subspecies. The Apache squirrel, *Sciurus apache*, is found in the mountains of southern Arizona. Commonly called the Chiricahua red squirrel, the Apache is considered a fox squirrel by Arizona authorities and is typical of the southern fox squirrel family.

The tree squirrel family is certainly large and varied, and hunters and wildlife watchers have plenty to keep them occupied during days afield. Of the squirrels that stand tall in the ranks of America's game animals—the eastern and western gray squirrels, the fox squirrel, the Arizona gray and Abert—the eastern gray leads the pack, but the others enjoy strong regional support.

Chapter

2

THE SQUIRREL'S WORLD

*B*oom! The echoes of the old scattergun's report ring out through the deep woods. A strained silence follows. Even the melodious music of the songbirds seems to stop on broken-off notes.

A tanned young face peers anxiously from behind a big white oak, two sharp eyes glued on the twitching gray form clinging precariously to the crotch of a sturdy hickory. Will it lodge in that crotch, requiring an early morning scramble up the tree to retrieve the prize? The barefoot boy in his early teens shivers slightly—partly from the nip of the cool dawn air of autumn, but also from excitement and the jolting recoil of the battered shotgun, which is the farm chicken hawk gun. Its recoil matches the legendary kick of the mule now grazing peacefully in the nearby pasture.

Finally the dying squirrel loses its grip on the bark of the aging tree and hits the leaf-covered ground with a resounding thump. The young hunter watches to make sure it lies motionless, marks the spot, and then settles back for another customer.

Our young hunter, though dressed poorly for the early morning chill, is cashing in on a well-planned hunt. It is no accident that he is within shotgun range of the nut-rich hickory tree at first light, the prime time to catch squirrels racing to their favorite trees for a dawn feast of tasty hickory nuts. He had located that hickory earlier in the summer as he took a shortcut home from a favorite fishing hole. Squirrels had already begun to gnaw on the still-green hickory nuts, and he knew that by the time the early squirrel season opened this would be a prime spot for him to bag his limit of fat bushytails.

He had laid his clothing out the night before, borrowed his dad's old shotgun, and stuffed a half dozen or so No. 6 shotshells into his pants pockets. It had been pitch dark when the alarm blared, but he had crawled out of his warm bed, dressed in the dark, and left the house in a jiffy. Dawn was just breaking as he had slipped into the hickory grove and assumed his vigil behind the big oak.

Young nimrods often start their hunting careers in the squirrel woods.

His wait had been brief.

This is squirrel hunting in the South, a tradition shared by many generations of country boys. Mornings like this one have started thousands of young men on hunting lives that later took them around the world in quest of larger, more exciting game. And lessons learned in the squirrel woods have served them well on all those subsequent hunts.

But in spite of later success with more challenging game, a seasoned squirrel hunter rarely shakes off the appeal of the squirrel woods, and intermittent trips to likely hickory groves sprinkle many long and varied hunting careers.

The gray, or cat, squirrel is the usual quarry of the southern hunter, though fox squirrels are popular in some areas where they are abundant enough to justify the hunter's time. Late August and early September have long been the accepted months to

Cracked hickory nuts are evidence that a squirrel fed here.

hunt squirrels in the South and across much of its wide range. However, the emphasis is gradually shifting to October and even November as modern wildlife managers now frown on early squirrel seasons.

The attraction of the early season for hunters is the squirrel's feeding activity in those months. This is "nut cutting" time. Hickory nuts still cling to the trees, and bushytails have to raid the tips of the branches to reap the harvest. Swaying tree branches and the sounds of sharp teeth literally cutting nuts loose from their stems, along with the rain of nut fragments, give away their presence. The hunter who chooses a good stand site can have a ball and then head home early with a limit of tasty squirrels.

This is also the season when ripe corn swells to full growth and the kernels harden on the ear. Fox squirrels, in particular, like to raid the ripening fields of corn, much to the dismay of the unfortunate farmer who has so carefully cultivated a fine crop. The hunter, taking his stand at dawn or dusk near the edge of a ripe cornfield, will likely harvest his limit in a hurry—and earn the gratitude of the farmer.

Switch the scene to the rugged mountains of West Virginia. The gray squirrel is one of the leading game animals in the Mountaineer State.

It is still dark when a couple of high-school boys park their dilapidated pickup truck on a wide shoulder of the highway, tuck light rifles under their arms, and head quickly up the mountain. It's mid-October and the autumn foliage is at its peak of color. Judging from the youngsters' quick steps over the rough terrain you would never guess that they had played leading roles in their football team's victory the evening before. But that was Friday, a day for football. This is Saturday, a time reserved for squirrel hunting.

Partway up the steep slope they pause briefly, confer for a minute or two, and then separate. They will each work a side of the mountain and meet later at a spot they are both familiar with.

Squirrel hunting has long been popular in West Virginia, with October being a top month. The hunting continues into the New Year, and state game managers at one time were experimenting with a September season. Squirrel hunting competes with the more glamorous pursuit of grouse and turkey for time in the hunter's schedule, not to mention the whitetail, but the bushytail holds its own in the eyes of the sharpshooting mountain men. The little .22-caliber rifle is a favorite firearm, but the scattergun, bow and arrow, and muzzleloader all get plenty of use in the vast West Virginia squirrel woods.

Meanwhile, in the deep woods of Maine a pair of grouse hunters are carefully working a likely covert. A flash of action catches the eye of one of the bird hunters. Instinctively, he swings his light scattergun over the possible target, but recognizing the bushy tail of a scampering squirrel, he lowers his shotgun and goes back to his partridge hunting. Maine hunters have shown little interest in bushytail over the years, despite the fact that squirrels are plentiful in the southern part of the state.

The same holds true for Connecticut, Massachusetts, New Hampshire, and Vermont, although wildlife managers feel that interest in squirrel hunting will gradually increase, particularly if the numbers of more popular species of game animals and birds decline. Vermont now holds a spring squirrel season. While there are good hardwood forests and prime squirrel cover all over New England, only in tiny Rhode Island are many hunters showing an interest in squirrel hunting.

Now, let's take a springtime visit to the Ozarks. Old-time Missouri squirrel hunters packed their game in a tin bucket and considered their hunt a success only when the pail was filled with fat

While squirrel hunting has a long history in the South, hunters in the Northeast are still discovering how much fun it is.

squirrels. But what about the Ozarks early in the twenty-first century? Missouri hunters currently bag between one and three million squirrels annually and the game is still underharvested. The season is long in Missouri, one reason for the heavy harvest. It begins in late May and runs for seven long months, ending in January. The first fifteen days of the season are considered the best, with the middle of August through October taking second place.

Spring squirrel hunting is becoming increasingly popular with seasons now open in Arkansas, Kentucky, Missouri, Oklahoma, Texas, and Vermont. Squirrels reproduce twice a year, and a spring season can be wedged between the breeding seasons. It provides a unique kind of hunting at a refreshing time of year to be in the woods.

Midwestern hunters avidly seek both fox and gray squirrels. The shaggy fox squirrels seem to be more abundant in the Mid-

The fox squirrel is slower than the little gray squirrel, but Midwestern hunters give it a lot of attention.

west than they are in other parts of their wide range. Half the hunters in Illinois say they hunt squirrels.

According to Charles Shick, game biologist for the Michigan Department of Natural Resources, hunters in that northern state consider fox and gray squirrel hunting to be great sport. He predicted several years ago that fox squirrel hunting would continue unchanged, but that the gray squirrel population might drop off because of the loss of habitat. Jack G. Mell, a Michigan outdoor writer, said the little animals were hunted heavily in his area.

Charles Nixon of the Ohio Department of Natural Resources, basing his position on the number of hunters who pursued them, said that squirrels were the most important forest game in the Buckeye State. Jack Connor, veteran Minnesota writer, told me his readers considered the squirrel a very desirable game animal.

A notable exception to the popularity of taking gray and fox squirrels across much of the country is found in the arid state of Arizona, where the long-eared Abert has long been considered a favorite of local hunters who go after them with the little .22-caliber rifle and a 4-power telescopic sight. Among the ponderosa pines of the Long Valley–Mongollon Rim, squirrel hunting is a popular sport that has attracted national attention. Dropping an Abert squirrel from the top of a tall pine tree with a little .22-caliber rifle can be a real hunting challenge.

TREE SQUIRREL DISTRIBUTION

The range of the eastern gray squirrel blankets the east half of the United States. Starting near the rocky coast of northern Maine, it extends to the tip of Florida and westward along the coast of the Gulf of Mexico to the eastern half of Texas. It then swings up to the northwestern corner of Minnesota, dips into Canada, and fol-

EASTERN
GRAY SQUIRREL
RANGE

lows the United States–Canadian border to Maine. Not a single eastern state is without a few bushytails to add some cheer to its woodlands.

While there has been little or no effort to stock squirrels, or to introduce them to new areas, a few gray squirrels exist in city parks far beyond their natural range. The little peanut-crunchers are found in many municipal parks in the western states, where only the western gray and little pine squirrels occur naturally.

The range of the big fox squirrel is much the same as that of the more popular gray, though in very little of this vast area is the fox as abundant. Generally, the fox's range starts a bit more to the south but extends much farther west than that of the gray.

The fox squirrel's range generally begins in southern New Jersey and, like the gray, runs south along the coast to the tip of Florida. It also extends along the Gulf Coast into Texas, but encompasses more of the Lone Star State, running along the Rio

FOX SQUIRREL
RANGE

Grande River and shooting north through the Panhandle to claim most of Oklahoma, Kansas, Nebraska, and South Dakota. From a point midway in South Dakota, it runs eastward through Minnesota, the Lower Peninsula of Michigan, Ohio, and the southern edge of Pennsylvania.

The range of the western gray is extremely limited, as the big squirrel is found only in the Pacific coast states of California, Oregon, and Washington. The world of the Arizona gray is also a small one. Found only in Arizona and New Mexico, it is fairly common in the former but is limited to the river bottoms of the southwestern part of the latter.

Also confined to the states of Arizona and New Mexico is the range of the Abert squirrel. Its Arizona territory covers practically all of the pine forests of the state, and even extends to areas that are isolated from other stands of timber. The New Mexico

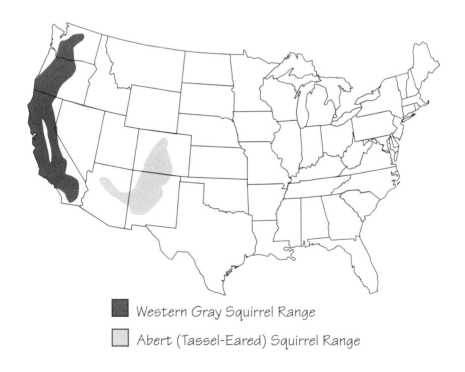

■ Western Gray Squirrel Range

□ Abert (Tassel-Eared) Squirrel Range

Abert lives primarily in the northwestern part of the state and in the more mountainous areas. The closely related Kaibab lives only in the Kaibab National Forest north of Arizona's famed Grand Canyon. Since hunting in the park is illegal, this squirrel is not considered a game species.

The range of the little red squirrel is truly a sprawling one, extending across the northern tier of states but bypassing the Great Plains and the Pacific Northwest. It dips into the Southland by following the evergreen forests south along the Appalachian Mountains into northern Georgia. The red is found throughout most of Canada and ranges into the rich forests of Alaska—the only squirrel native to the forty-ninth state. In the West, its range follows the coniferous forests of the northern Rockies south into Arizona and New Mexico.

The chickaree, or Douglas squirrel, is found in a very limited area of the United States, filling the void left in the Pacific Northwest by the red squirrel. Located primarily in California, Oregon, and Washington, the chickaree is also reported in Arizona, Colorado, Idaho, Nevada, New Mexico, and Utah.

Found throughout the eastern half of the United States, with the possible exception of Maine and the northernmost areas of states along the Canadian border, the southern flying squirrel seems to be inappropriately named. The western boundary for the range of this night-loving member of the squirrel family is a line running roughly from a point midway on the Texas coast to western Minnesota.

The northern flying squirrel's range is more limited in the United States, but it covers all of Canada except the plains provinces. In the United States it follows both major mountain ranges and the Pacific Coast south into California, Colorado, and Georgia. Otherwise, it is found only in the Northeast and in the timber-rich states along the Canadian border.

The range of the tree squirrels is varied and far-reaching, stretching from coast to coast and from the long Canadian border to Mexico and the Gulf of Mexico, which is one reason they make such popular targets for hunters.

Chapter

3

HABITAT

The tree squirrels are arboreal, adapted to life in forests primarily composed of hardwoods. Their ability to scamper from one swaying tree branch to another, often from one tree to another, is a major defense against predators. Trees provide the squirrel with nuts and buds for food and cavities and dens for shelter. Trees of one kind or another are vital to the squirrels' survival, hence the name tree squirrel.

EASTERN GRAY COUNTRY

The preferred habitat of the eastern gray, one of the most common of our tree squirrels, is difficult to pin down due to the variety of places it calls home. The fact that the gray is so widely distributed attests to its adaptability.

Early settlers to the shores of America found the eastern half of the new continent covered with vast hardwoods, rich in mast and sprinkled liberally with aged oaks that supplied an abundance of dens for squirrels and other wildlife. Such a setup is ideal for the gray squirrel. It prefers the dense woods and heavily forested areas—big timber with lots of shade and an understory of small trees and shrubs, plus den trees for nesting and rearing its young.

The gray squirrel is at home in dense hardwood forests.

The woodsman's axe, rather than the hunter's rifle, has been the real culprit in reducing what was once a thriving gray squirrel population in the eastern United States. These vast virgin forests have paid a heavy price in the name of progress.

Despite the loss of so much of its preferred habitat, the gray squirrel has displayed an amazing ability to adapt to man's ways and hang on in the face of encroaching civilization. Today the gray squirrel is found in farm woodlots, city parks, and the afflu-ent suburbs of America, as well as remaining stands of hardwood forest.

When den trees are scarce it nests in gutters, attics, bird-houses, beneath the eaves of houses, and anywhere else it can find reasonable protection from the weather. The squirrel's nat-ural enemies are not as prevalent under such conditions as they are in its preferred habitat. Outwitting the alley cat or the neighbor's dog is no problem for the nimble bushytail.

Squirrels are omnivorous. They eat both plant and animal matter, but their primary diet comes from plants. The list of natural foods utilized by the gray squirrel is almost endless. Its favorite choices are acorns, chestnuts, and hickory nuts, but it also eats hazelnuts, wild cherries, poplar cones, buds, fruits, berries, insects, mushrooms, field corn, peanuts, beechnuts, wild grapes, walnuts, Osage orange, garden vegetables, bulbs, seeds of hornbeam, dogwood, bittersweet, black gum, smartweed, cypress, pinecones, butternuts, pecans, cedar berries, tubers, and the eggs of frogs, lizards, and birds.

Under ideal conditions, the home range of the gray squirrel may be 100 to 150 acres. Good squirrel habitat contains from five

All the squirrels are attracted to nut trees.

to a dozen mast-producing trees per acre; a well-fed squirrel consumes its own weight in food every week.

Mass migrations of squirrels, observed often in earlier days, are believed to have been caused by shortages of food. Even today, there is substantial evidence that squirrels migrate in search of food. Smart hunters recognize this trend. Squirrels, however, are no longer abundant enough for these migrations to reach mass proportions.

While the gray is found in mixed hardwood forests throughout its range—be it mountains, valleys, or rolling hills—it seems to be most abundant in creek and river bottoms and in swamps containing good stands of hardwoods. It shuns the high country. In West Virginia, for example, probably the most mountainous state in the eastern gray's wide range, this squirrel is seldom found at elevations in excess of 3,000 feet. One reason for this is the scarcity of hardwoods at higher elevations.

In Texas and other southern states, the gray is seldom found in upland forests, but it seems to find the higher land more acceptable in the North, possibly because swamplands are not as plentiful. Hammocks—a combination of oak, sweet gum, black gum, elm, red mulberry, magnolia, holly, ironwood, hornbeam, yaupon, beech, huckleberry, pecan, hickory, and some pine—make ideal habitat from Texas to Florida in the Deep South. Spanish moss and vines make excellent escape cover. And the greater the variety of vines, trees, and shrubs, the better the habitat.

The gray squirrel's yen for burying nuts for winter use helps preserve its habitat, as many of these nuts are never recovered; instead, they sprout to create new trees. The squirrel has long been considered a boon to reforestation.

The squirrel's enemies are many. They include the larger hawks and owls, weasels, minks, foxes, bobcats, snakes, and domestic cats and dogs. In recent years, a growing bald eagle popu-

A busy squirrel digs for a nut it buried here during the peak of the season. (Joel Arrington)

lation in some areas represents a threat to squirrels. But an alert and agile squirrel knows how to use its environment for protection. In good health and in its preferred habitat, the gray squirrel does not suffer significantly from predation.

Aged trees in mature forests contain many hollows and cavities that make ideal squirrel dens. When left unmolested, nature works in many ways to build these dens. Bolts of lightning crack the trunks of tall oaks and decay eventually sets in. Strong winds rip branches from trees, exposing the inner tree and inviting decay. Lower limbs in well-shaded forests die and drop off, and decay often commences before the opening heals over. Woodpeckers also contribute to the squirrel's cause, hammering away at those scars in their constant search for food. It may take ten to fifteen years for a good den site to develop from such a natural cavity.

Black gum, beech, maple, black cherry, black oak, white oak, red oak, scarlet oak, chestnut oak, hickory, sycamore, and tuliptree are among the best den-producing trees. The trunk of a good den tree will be at least ten inches in diameter.

In areas where natural dens aren't available, the gray builds leaf nests in the crotches of trees. Though not as cozy as a good den, the leaf nest serves the squirrel well in warmer climates. Summer litters are often reared in leaf nests. These nests are usually built of twigs, leaves, and sticks and are lined with bark, cornhusks, grass, and even paper. They are easy to spot on scouting walks through the woods, particularly after the leaves are down in autumn.

Once destroyed, good squirrel habitat is not easily or quickly restored. It can be had for a price—work and patience. But it is impossible to start from scratch and produce good

Good squirrel habitat includes a selection of mature hardwoods.

squirrel habitat overnight. The task more nearly approaches a lifetime undertaking.

David M. Christisen, biologist with the Missouri Department of Conservation once estimated that a thirty-five-year-old man who plants a barren field with tree seedlings cannot expect to see good squirrel habitat in his lifetime. His ten-year-old son will just begin to see a few squirrels and great potentialities before he dies. The planter's grandson, finally, will likely be amazed by the large and thriving squirrel population.

The destiny of the gray squirrel lies mostly in the hands of forest and timber interests. If they exercise wise management on their timber holdings, harvesting the trees selectively and leaving mast and den trees for the squirrel's food and home, the future of the bushytail is bright. And habitat that is good for the gray squirrel is advantageous for turkey, deer, and other forest game that also need mature hardwoods for survival.

FOX COUNTRY

Second in importance from the hunter's standpoint is the big fox squirrel, which in some parts of the country is more abundant than the gray. The fox squirrel isn't nearly so demanding in its habitat requirements. It shuns the deep woods, the mature and dense forests so attractive to the gray. Instead, it likes the forest edges, the mature hedgerows, small woodlots with openings in the canopy, and the scattering of trees in park-like pastures. The fox also shows a preference for ridges.

Less ground cover is necessary for the fox squirrel. In fact, light livestock grazing in woodlots with an open canopy seems to benefit the fox squirrel by holding the understory plants in check. Mature hardwood lots of mast-bearing species are characteristic of fox squirrel habitat. Mixed stands of oak are excellent, but approximately ten acres of forest is optimum, as opposed to the

Fox squirrels are often found in semi-open cover along forest edges.

gray's preference for vast stands of dense forests. Ideally, cover lanes such as hedges or thickets along fencerows will connect the woodlots.

While the fox and gray squirrels will tolerate each other, this difference in habitat requirements limits one or the other in any particular locality. Timber harvesting may drive out the gray by opening up the cover, only to create an area more attractive to the fox. This happened years ago in the Lower Peninsula of Michigan. Early settlers removed the dense forests through logging, fires, and development. The gray squirrel populations almost disappeared, but the fox squirrel found the woodlots and surrounding farmlands to its liking. As a result, the fox has flourished in this region.

In a squirrel study several years ago, the Missouri Department of Conservation found that the total squirrel harvest was split 51 percent for fox squirrels and 49 percent for gray squirrels.

On the basis of habitat, the fox squirrel bag from the prairies was 66 percent and from the forests it was 39 percent. Additionally, it was discovered that hunters bagged a much higher proportion of adult fox squirrels than young in the forests, but on the prairies the ratio conformed to typical standards of over 50 percent juveniles.

The fox squirrel finds forests of tall, mature pine acceptable as a home. In fact, North Carolina biologists believe that early logging operations in their state, which were particularly heavy in virgin pine forests, took an earlier and heavier toll on fox squirrels than on grays. Today, the habitat of the fox squirrel in North Carolina is mostly limited to eastern stands of pines mixed with a few hardwoods.

Out in Colorado, where the fox squirrel is not a native, it has accepted streams bordered by cottonwoods and willows as satisfactory habitat.

Much like the gray, the fox also prefers a tree cavity for its den. Favorites for this purpose are beech, oak, elm, sycamore, and maple. In the absence of satisfactory den trees, however, it will build a nest in the crotch of a tall tree. The nest is typically round or oval in shape and tightly woven of fresh-cut hardwood twigs. Inside, a layer of

A big fox squirrel poses near its den in an oak tree.

tightly compressed leaves forms a rigid wall. The wall is then lined with shredded bark or other soft material and has a single opening for an entry. The nest is placed so that it gets the utmost protection from wind and rain. The fox squirrel's nest averages twelve to thirty inches in diameter, with an inner cavity of six to eight inches.

The home range of the fox squirrel is considerably smaller than that of the gray, often as little as two hundred yards in diameter. A population of two fox squirrels per acre is considered high.

The food list of the fox squirrel is also a long one, including the usual nuts, tree buds in the spring, berries, mushrooms, and insects. Not surprisingly, acorns and hickory nuts are the common mainstay. The fox, however, is more inclined to feed on agricultural products such as corn, barley, wheat, or other grains. In fact, in some parts of its range—in Colorado, for example—it is often primarily dependent on agricultural residue. This is also true in Nebraska and other states near the western extreme of the fox squirrel's range, where hardwood forests are sparser.

In corn country, the fox squirrel feeds heavily on this crop and often lives near the edges of cornfields. In Indiana, husky three-pound fox squirrels have been routed from corncribs where they were wintering in the lap of luxury. While much of the blame for such crop destruction falls on the diminutive back of the fox squirrel, raccoons and other animals and birds are often the culprits.

Explorers drifting westward from the Ohio River only found fox squirrels on the prairies, where they lived in trees scattered along the fringes. However, as forests were cut and burned in other areas, the fox squirrel moved in. Somewhere between solid virgin forests and total timber destruction, a favorable balance of cover enabled the fox to achieve pest-sized populations in Indiana and other Midwestern states.

As discussed above, both fox and gray squirrels utilize leaf nests in the absence of den trees. But leaf nests provide only marginal protection for young squirrels born during cold-weather months—as early as February and March in some areas. The lack of hollow trees for nesting is probably equally as damaging to squirrel populations as the cutting of food trees during logging operations.

The fox is more ground-oriented than the gray, spending less of its time in the treetops of America. It seems to prefer the higher ridges over the bottomlands. The fox squirrel is also a poor harvester, relying instead on a layer of fat to get it through the winter months. In Florida, it prefers the open piney woods, where it feeds heavily on pine seeds.

The fox squirrel adapts well to farmland and woodlot.

While the replacement of dense forests by open fields and woodlots would seem to favor the broad extension of its range into much of the United States, fox squirrel populations have not grown to any degree except in the Midwestern and prairie states. Perhaps limited stocking would establish this big squirrel in other parts of the country, where the changing forest picture seems better suited to its needs than those of the gray.

WESTERN GRAY COUNTRY

Unlike the smaller eastern gray squirrel, the big western gray prefers the high country. In California they are found at elevations of 2,000 to 3,000 feet, although they also live in the oak woodland areas in the valleys and foothills. The higher elevations are part of the Cascade and Sierra Mountain Ranges. The Oregon Cascade Mountains also harbor a good population of western grays, as do the eastern slopes of Mount Hood.

They live in forests in these mountainous areas, making their homes in hollow trees. But like the other major tree squirrels they build nests of twigs and leaves about thirty feet above the ground when suitable den trees aren't present. They thrive in oak

Checking for squirrel sign on a winter hunt.

and fir forests and nut-growing agricultural regions. In some areas, the big gray often becomes a real pest to the nut grower and farmer.

In addition to agricultural crops, the western gray feeds on acorns, mushrooms, pine nuts, seeds, filberts, walnuts, and occasionally insect larvae and small birds or carrion.

Predators include hawks, owls, coyotes, foxes, and bobcats, although the western gray's numbers are not significantly affected by predation. Disease is of greater concern, as it can make the western gray more susceptible to predation by weakening it to the point where it can no longer take full advantage of its habitat.

ABERT COUNTRY

The tassel-eared, or Abert, squirrel spends most of its life in the ponderosa pine forests of the Southwest. It is found in most of the pine forests of Arizona and in many isolated woodlots far from major forests. It, too, likes the high country—the rugged mountains of Arizona, Colorado, and New Mexico.

While the Abert squirrel may occasionally build a den in a cottonwood or oak tree, hollows are rare in ponderosa pines. More often, this tassel-eared member of the tree squirrel clan will

Abert squirrels love the tall ponderosa pines of the Southwest. (Bob Whitaker)

resort to a nest in the crotch of a tree. The nest is usually fashioned of interlocked branches and twigs and heavily thatched leaves. Soft bark and plant fiber line the center of the living space, making the nest warm and comfortable. The nest usually has several entrances.

The Abert's diet is a varied one, depending to a large degree upon what nature provides in the greatest abundance. Foods in the forest range from nuts and seeds to mushrooms and fungi. The male flowers, or staminate catkins, of the ponderosa pine are a favorite food for young squirrels. They also feed on the cambium (inner bark) of the pine tree.

During the autumn of a good pinecone-production year the Abert squirrel will perch in the tree branches and leisurely pull the scales off the cones as he scratches for the seeds within. Acorn crops are somewhat rare in the Southwest, but scattered oaks do grow in the pine forests, and oak mast is another favorite when available.

Water is a scarce item in the normal habitat of the Abert, and the squirrel seems to take most of its water from the food it eats. It drinks freely, however, when water is readily available.

The Abert's habit of cutting bough tips to obtain the inner bark has alienated a few cattlemen in its range. The freshly cut pine twigs fall to the ground and a certain chemical change occurs, making them palatable to cattle by increasing the sugar content. Unfortunately, the twigs apparently contain substances which, when digested, cause miscarriages. Often, the cow dies along with the newborn calf.

OTHER TREE SQUIRREL COUNTRY

The Arizona gray squirrel, limited in its range, is an inhabitant of the river bottoms and canyons of the Southwest—primarily Arizona and New Mexico. Its food habits parallel those of the Abert, though the Arizona black walnut is a highly favored food when present.

The Apache squirrel of southern Arizona is at home in the mountains of that section of the state. Its habitat requirements are much like those of the big fox squirrel discussed earlier in this chapter.

The red, pine, or spruce squirrel is an inhabitant of the high country, and coniferous forests are its preferred habitat. These tiny squirrels can squeeze into small holes and utilize all kinds of tree cavities to build their nests of leaves and twigs. Given the opportunity, the little red squirrel will chase a woodpecker out of its woodland house and move right in. It feeds on seeds, nuts, fruit, cones, insects, mushrooms, and occasionally eggs.

Fortunately, few forests across North America are without at least a few bushytails. A forest without squirrels is a sad place, indeed.

Chapter
4

METHODS OF HUNTING

The various hunting tactics that can be employed on the popular bushytail no doubt contribute considerably to its lofty ranking among the game animals of America. The rifleman, shotgunner, archer, and black-powder enthusiast all find the squirrel a worthy quarry. Even the hunter who likes to use trail and treeing hounds will find that the squirrel fits into his plans.

SCOUTING

As is true in most forms of hunting, a certain amount of scouting prior to the hunt will save untold amounts of wasted time afield and increase the nimrod's chances of success. Squirrel sign is not difficult to detect. Look for fragments of cracked nuts under hickory, oak, and beech trees or chewed-up pinecones in the vicinity of evergreens. Squirrels also perch on rocks or stumps to eat, leaving little piles of nut remains. In Abert squirrel habitat, look for scattered seeds or buds of ponderosa pine.

Scratch marks on tree trunks and bark that looks like it has been chewed on are also good signs. Squirrel scat is usually hard to find in the squirrel woods, and it's not really necessary to look for it.

A great variety of methods can be employed to hunt squirrels, which is probably one of the reasons hunters like them so much.

If ripe fields of corn are available during the hunting season, scout the edges next to hardwoods and look for chewed-on ears of corn or scattered grain. The owner of the cornfield will likely welcome the opportunity to have the squirrel population thinned out a bit.

If you scout in early morning or late afternoon you can often observe feeding squirrels and use their movements to pinpoint their feeding trees, their den trees, and their likely routes of approach. Squirrels often travel on established pathways through the treetops that allow them to move quickly between feeding and denning areas. Identify these corridors while scouting and you may have an easier time spotting game on future hunts in the area.

When snow is on the ground in winter, or in muddy areas, squirrels can be located by their tracks. They are easy to identify

Scattered nut fragments are always clear signs of squirrel activity.

Spotting squirrels and studying their movements will tell you a lot about their favorite areas.

after a little practice. All the squirrels have four toes on the forefeet and five on the hind feet—unlike raccoons and opossums, which have five toes on all four feet. The hind print of a gray squirrel usually runs 2¼ to 2½ inches long, while the front track is shorter at around 1¼ inches. The tracks of fox squirrels usually run slightly larger. Chipmunks and mice also have four toes up front and five in the back, but their tracks are noticeably smaller.

Other clues can also help you distinguish squirrel tracks from other animals of the forest. For instance, the tracks may lead to and from trees where dens are present or where other signs of

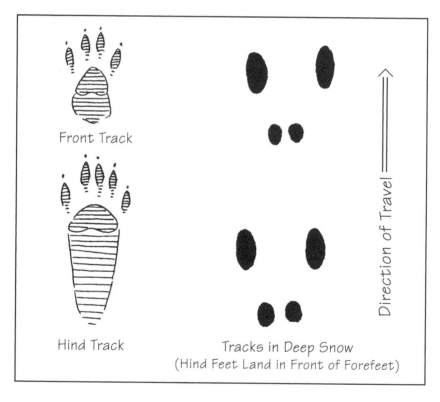

Front Track

Hind Track

Tracks in Deep Snow
(Hind Feet Land in Front of Forefeet)

Direction of Travel

Gray Squirrel Tracks

squirrel activity are obvious. If you're in prime gray squirrel habitat and all the other signs match, you're probably looking at the tracks of a gray.

Even when you don't see squirrels out and about while scouting, it pays to keep your eyes open for den trees. Binoculars are very useful for locating dens and examining them up close for signs of recent use. Active dens are well worn and the bark around the den entrance is scratched from the squirrels' claws. The presence of leaf nests is another good squirrel sign, and these are usually easy to spot.

Once the squirrels' hangouts are located through scouting, the actual hunting trip is reduced to getting on a good stand well before the peak of activity and then waiting for the fun to begin or still-hunting through quality habitat.

The well-worn entrance to a squirrel den near the base of an oak.

STILL-HUNTING AND STAND HUNTING

The successful hunter must overcome the squirrel's keen ears, sharp vision, and natural elusiveness. The squirrel's sense of smell is also surprisingly strong. The animal often digs through six inches of snow to locate buried nuts, but it probably uses this sense more for locating cached food than as a defense against its enemies, After all, a squirrel perched high in the crotch of a tall oak is in no position to detect the odor of a hunter moving slowly across the forest floor. Still, some hunters like to work into or across the wind to eliminate any possibility of their scent being carried to the quarry.

It takes good woodsmanship on the part of the hunter to enable him or her to overcome the squirrel's sense of hearing. The squirrel hunter should steal a page from the big-game hunter's book and learn to move silently and slowly. He should select his route carefully, and not attempt to stalk and hunt at the same time. Instead, the hunter should concentrate on moving noiselessly with his eyes to the ground, pausing frequently to study his

These three gray squirrels were taken while they fed in a hickory tree. A careful hunter can bring home a bag like this from a single stand.

surroundings for signs of game. In this way he can avoid a fatal step on dry twigs or leaves that may snap or rustle, telegraphing his presence to every squirrel in the vicinity.

The weather is an important factor in this regard. It's much easier to move silently when the forest floor is wet from a recent rain than when it's dry. Wet days, when a light drizzling rain drifts down from a gray sky, are one of my favorite times for squirrel hunting.

Camouflage, concealment, and cover help the hunter overcome the squirrel's excellent vision. However, from its vantage point high in a tree the squirrel has a tremendous advantage in sighting potential predators roaming down below.

The hunter should try to locate his quarry from a distance and keep its location well marked as he works within shooting range. He can use cliffs, ravines, hills, and other terrain features to conceal his approach. For short distances, it may be possible for the hunter to keep a large tree between himself and the squirrel as he moves cautiously into range, employing normal stalking tactics.

Heavy foliage can aid the hunter considerably during the early

The author uses a tree for cover as he keeps an eye on a moving gray squirrel.

season, though it works to the advantage of the squirrel, too. A feeding squirrel perched on a limb and chomping away on a nut is harder to locate through the thick leaf cover, although swaying tree branches will quickly betray any move it makes in the foliage.

The squirrel hunter who waits on a stand is not confronted with many of the problems that face the moving hunter. He sits or stands quietly, minimizing movement. He is not concerned about how he will approach his quarry. He simply waits for squirrels to come to him. A precautionary measure that may pay dividends is to clear loose leaves from around the stand so that an occasional shift in position will not rustle leaves or snap twigs.

By selecting his location carefully and wearing camouflage clothing, the stand hunter can make himself nearly invisible to squirrels in the vicinity. If a good position is taken up in prime habitat, there should be plenty of action. Smart hunters scout out

This Georgia hunter has taken a stand near a prime den site. (Aaron Pass)

several good stand sites and move to them as conditions dictate during the day.

Regardless of the method used, the prime hunting hours are early and late in the day. The gray squirrel is usually up at dawn and on its way to a good nut tree. The fox squirrel may sleep a little later, but it's often up and moving before the average hunter's day begins, too. Squirrels also feed late in the day, starting to move about by late afternoon and continuing until dark. The experienced squirrel hunter, however, usually considers the early morning hours better than late afternoon. The most success comes during those peak hours.

Unfortunately, such hours don't fit the average American's daily routine of breakfast at 7 or 8 AM and dinner at 5 to 7 PM. Some sacrifice may be necessary to get into the woods at the best times for hunting.

My own approach is to arise before daylight, hunt until breakfast, devote the day to work or other activities, and then spend another hour or so in the squirrel woods after dinner. Luckily, the best squirrel hunting usually occurs during the fall months when the days are still reasonably long.

A few squirrels remain active throughout

A successful squirrel hunter works the edge of a hardwood forest.

the day, and the persistent hunter is likely to score during those off-hours, even at midday. Sometimes squirrels seem to break with the norm and become active around 10 AM or just before noon. But the hunter's success rate won't be nearly as high as it is during the hours of peak squirrel activity.

The best hunters use the squirrel's daily routine—up and feeding at dawn, a snooze near midday, and another feed late in the day—to their advantage.

Harsh weather may cause the squirrel to vary its habits slightly. On rainy or extremely cold days it may feed earlier in the afternoon and later in the day. In fact, when it's rainy and overcast, squirrels may feed at various times throughout the day.

Squirrel-hunting seasons vary throughout the country, and hunting methods must be adjusted according to prevailing conditions. Long before game officials even considered regulations for governing the harvest of squirrels, late summer and early fall emerged as the most lucrative season to harvest them. Why? The bushytail is busy cutting nuts that cling to the trees at this time of year, and they are active and easier to spot.

Once the hunter finds a hickory tree laden with nuts, hunting can be as easy as getting on a stand before daylight and waiting for game to appear. In good fox squirrel country the border of a ripe cornfield might replace the hickory tree.

Although squirrels are harder to locate when the foliage is heavy, it's possible to read the signs that betray a squirrel's presence. One is the unusual movement of tree branches. With a little practice, it is easy to distinguish the movement of a leafy branch giving way beneath the weight of a squirrel from more natural movement caused by the wind.

Another good indication of a squirrel's presence during a hunt—one that requires good ears—is the sound of falling nut fragments. Feeding squirrels love to perch on a high limb and

With one fox squirrel in the bag, the author waits patiently for another from a good stand.

chomp away at green hickory nuts. The sound of the chips and fragments filtering through the leafy branches can be quite loud. Once the hunter zeroes in on this activity, he can study the tree carefully until his target is located.

Squirrels also feed on acorns in late summer through fall, but the big hickory nuts seem to hold a special charm for them. If you can find them congregating in hickory groves and actively feeding on the nuts, stand hunting is usually the best option. But when squirrels feed on acorns they move around a lot because the nuts are typically more scattered, which means that stalking or even using a dog might be more effective.

Summer hunting is still legal and popular in many sections of the best bushytail country. The blind or stand is the most effective method of taking squirrels at this time of year, because feeding areas are easy to locate.

To hunt an area most efficiently, it's important to first make a plan of attack.

Later in the fall, hickory trees become bare of nuts and the stand hunter has to adjust his methods. As winter approaches squirrels feed on the hearts of pinecones, acorns, and other available nuts. Once the hunter has determined what squirrels are eating at a specific time he can continue hunting successfully from a stand.

During the fall and winter squirrels become more gregarious, and several may use the same den tree. The hunter who locates such a tree can enjoy some fast shooting for a few minutes after dawn and again just at dusk as the squirrels return for the night. This type of hunting is extremely limited, though, as the productive periods may last only a half hour or so.

Whether it is summer, fall or winter, the successful stand hunter must learn to sit quietly and wait patiently for his game to appear. Like most animals on a feeding jaunt, squirrels usually move slowly and sporadically along the ground or through the trees, and there is no way to hurry them along. The comfortable, relaxed hunter will be able to wait out the squirrels much more quietly and enjoy the experience more than one who is tense or in a cramped position. So it's important to take steps to ensure that the stand site is comfortable and void of anything that might lead to loud noises, even if you're just sitting on the ground and leaning back against a stout tree.

Stands need not be fancy, but they should be comfortable.

Another practice that pays off for the stand hunter is resisting the urge to recover fallen game immediately. Squirrels often play and move in pairs or trios. The sharp report of a small-caliber rifle is less likely to alarm the squirrel population than a hunter's movements. When the game drops to the forest floor, the hunter should mark its location, assure himself that it is dead, and remain on his stand. Within fifteen or twenty minutes—and possibly sooner—the squirrels will be feeding or playing again and the hunter will get another chance.

Sometimes, instead of running from danger a squirrel may freeze against a tree, its gray hair blending with the bark. Only an

If you're on a productive stand, wait until the hunt is finished before picking up fallen game.

experienced and sharp-sighted hunter can locate such a squirrel. Instead of looking for the squirrel's entire body, train yourself to watch for smaller things that seem slightly out of place. For instance, a squirrel's ears often give it away.

When time constraints and/or prevailing conditions don't permit scouting trips—and this is often the case with casual hunters—the best approach is to still-hunt or stalk until game is located and then switch to stand hunting. Some hunters use the trout fisherman's trick of opening the stomach of the first squirrel bagged in an effort to determine what they are feeding on. However, to do this successfully the hunter must be able to identify squirrel foods by their smell as well as their appearance.

Both the fox and gray squirrels have a tendency to work toward the outer edges of woodlots as they feed on nuts in small forested areas. In places like this the stalking hunter can sometimes net good results by just walking slowly around the edge of the woods, pausing often to study the tree canopies and the ground ahead.

Hunting seasons in late summer and early fall are gradually losing favor among game managers around the country. They feel that too many young squirrels are robbed of their mothers as the summer offspring are still nursing at this time. Many hunters agree.

Another objection to warm-weather hunting stems from the botflies that infest the game at this time. While they do not affect the meat, their presence makes many hunters squeamish about eating their kill. The result is that valuable game is left in the woods to rot or be consumed by scavengers.

Pause often while still-hunting to check the surrounding cover for game.

Most biologists and serious hunters recommend late fall, after the leaves have fallen, as the best time of year to hunt squirrels. The botflies are gone then, the young are on their own, and squirrels are easier to locate with the trees bare of foliage. This last point may be debatable, as an experienced hunter can locate a squirrel by the movement of tree branches, the sound of its bark, or feeding activities. And without the protection of the foliage the hunter finds it more difficult to conceal himself as he stalks his quarry. Also, squirrels do become more wary once the leaves are gone.

Like so many game species, squirrel populations reach their annual peak in October.

The author uses a big oak tree for concealment on a late-fall day after the leaves have fallen.

In any event, fall hunting methods are not much different from those used earlier in the season. Since the squirrel's feeding activities may be less concentrated, the stand method becomes of less value and more emphasis is placed on moving and stalking. Late and early vigils at well-used den trees can pay rich dividends.

HUNTING WITH DOGS

While I have never owned a squirrel dog, nor hunted behind one to any extent, I know a few fine sportsmen who do. They take pride in their squirrel dogs and derive a good deal of pleasure from watching them perform—locating, trailing, and treeing their game.

Many of the accepted squirrel-hunting principals go out the window when a dog is used. For example, there is no such thing as waiting in a blind with a squirrel dog. The dog is not noted for that kind of patience, and what good would it do the hunter anyway? Since the hunter relies on the dog to locate the game, he does not have to exercise the same degree of patience the still-hunter does. There is, however, no excuse for crashing wildly through the woods. Early morning and late afternoon vigils also become less important, as the dog is at its best when the game is scattered throughout the woods. This usually occurs later in the morning and earlier in the afternoon.

Many times while in the woods the bark of a dog has attracted my curiosity. When I find the dog I usually find a treed squirrel, too. All kinds of dogs engage in this kind of hunting—all too often unsupervised and unaccompanied by their owner. But the thing that has always impressed

Scouting takes a backseat when you're hunting with dogs, as they will do the work of actually locating squirrels.

me is the ease with which I can approach the tree and not frighten the treed squirrel. The presence of the barking dog seems to freeze the animal, and it either hugs the tree or dashes back and forth along a limb scolding its tormentor. The squirrel seems to know that its canine enemy doesn't present a serious threat so long as it remains aloft and beyond the range of the dog's outstretched jaws.

Even if the treed animal doesn't freeze for the dog, or dogs, it will certainly do so when the hunter arrives on the scene. Then locating the game can become a problem. On a windy day, the breeze ruffling the squirrel's bushy tail may give it away. Sometimes pounding on the tree trunk or shaking a small tree or vines nearby will make it move. When dogs are used, hunters should work in pairs—one to make the game move and the other to do the shooting.

Both bird dogs and beagles will tree squirrels if you don't want to keep a separate dog just for squirrels. I have had frisky bushytails interrupt both kinds of hunting—bunny-busting be-hind a pack of little beagles or shooting quail over a pair of setters.

I never get too disturbed when a beagle shows an interest in squirrels. They are trail hounds, and their interest in squirrels is usually a temporary whim. But when my prize bird dogs tree a squirrel I do get upset, because once they start it's hard to break them of the habit.

For example, I had a Gordon setter named Mike who was an excellent bird dog and an eager hunter. A friend borrowed Mike one day and as they skirted a stretch of hardwoods, Mike picked up a squirrel's scent, trailed it to a big oak, and treed it. He had done this to me on a number of occasions, but I had always or-dered him from the tree and refrained from shooting the squirrel. I didn't want to make a squirrel dog of my prize setter! However, I forgot to caution my friend on this point, and being a newcomer to quail hunting, he innocently dropped the squirrel with a well-placed load of birdshot.

Encouraged by the success of his find and my friend's shoot-ing, Mike became an incurable squirrel dog. He continued to find birds for me so long as I kept him in the field, but if I wanted to hunt near a woodlot he would invariably desert the quail for a go at the squirrels.

It is difficult to predict what kind of canine friend will make the best squirrel dog. Many kennels train and sell dogs for that specific purpose, though most owners probably come by their squirrel hunting dogs less formally. You can usually find ads from breeders in the major sporting magazines and by searching the Internet.

No particular breed seems to excel as a producer of squirrel dogs. The aforementioned beagle is a good choice, and seldom needs much training for squirrels. All he'll need is an understand-ing of basic commands. Just take a precocious pup into some woods with a good squirrel population and he will soon get the idea, particularly if you shoot a bushytail out of a tree for him.

Mixed breeds or mongrels often make better squirrel hunters than the purebreds, and there are a wide variety of cur and feist breeds that have strong squirrel-hunting reputations. Common sense — or dog sense — would point to the trail hounds as the best bets, but this is not always the case. One reason is that a squirrel dog hunts as much by sight as by smell. In fact, those that hunt by sight are usually more effective.

The ability to watch the treetops and follow a squirrel escaping to other trees is vital to the success of the operation. Experienced dogs remember this and do it instinctively. But as most dogs use both sight and sound, it pays to remember that the ground holds scent better when conditions are damp. Extremely dry weather makes picking up scent difficult on dogs.

A lone dog can often do the job better than two or more, as even a small pack of dogs quickly becomes a nuisance in the squirrel woods.

Late fall and winter are the preferred seasons

While a variety of dogs can be used to hunt squirrels, trail hounds are the choice of many hunters.

59

for employing dogs in the pursuit of squirrels. Food is more difficult to find. Most of the nuts have fallen from the trees. And old bushytail has to fan out more in search of his daily rations. This makes him more vulnerable to a roaming squirrel dog—not to mention easier to spot with the leaves down. Keep in mind that in a few states where spring hunting is allowed the use of dogs is not.

As is true of most hunts in which dogs are used, the squirrel hunter has to give his partner some guidance. This begins with putting the dog in a wooded area that is known to hold squirrels. If you've made some scouting trips, are knowledgeable about squirrel habit, and have the ability to spot signs of game such as nut cuttings and well-used dens this shouldn't be a problem.

These hounds have a squirrel treed, but that's no guarantee the hunter will get a great shot opportunity.

Once the dog is released in known squirrel habitat, you can rely on it to locate the game, though you should continue to direct the dog's hunting efforts by leading it to the most likely habitat. If a certain patch of woods proves fruitless, call in the dog and move to another location.

Just follow your canine ally until he strikes game. Then comes the chase, followed by the treeing. The chase is typically a short one, often just to the nearest sizable tree. You can usually tell by the change in the tune of a dog's bark when the chase is over and the game is treed.

A treed squirrel behaves differently than one jumped in the normal manner. Instead of darting for a den tree or scampering away through the treetops, a squirrel pursued by a dog is more likely to freeze against the tree, relying on its gray coat to blend into the bark of the tree, usually an oak. The camouflaged animal often looks like just another bump on the trunk or limb of the tree, and careful study is required to pick out its form. But as the dog is providing clear evidence of the squirrel's presence in the tree, it should be easier to stay focused on the search. And that extra bit of concentration will pay off.

I suppose that most hunters who hunt squirrels with dogs use a shotgun. After all, scatterguns and dogs fit together well in all types of small-game and bird hunts. Although many squirrels freeze when treed, a squirrel hopping about in the trees and carrying on a verbal battle with the dog on the ground is no target for the precision-shooting rifleman.

To my knowledge, the squirrel is the only small-game animal that can be successfully hunted with a treeing dog during daylight hours. It fills a unique void in small-game hunting. While opossums and raccoons are also hunted with treeing hounds, that is almost exclusively a night-hunting sport.

For gun hunters who don't like to leave their dogs at home, canines of all kinds can be surprisingly useful in the squirrel woods. Yet another reason this little game animal is so fun to hunt.

THE SQUIRREL CALL

Game calls of all kinds have become extremely popular in recent years. Crow calls, duck and goose calls, and turkey calls are the old favorites, but we now have a wide variety of game calls available that have been introduced to the American hunting scene by imaginative hunters and enterprising manufacturers. One of the most popular of the new arrivals is the varmint call, the eerie sounds of a dying rabbit. It calls coyotes, foxes, bobcats, and other predators to the hunter's gun or arrow.

The squirrel hunter has not been neglected, either. A squirrel call is most effective on young, curious animals. There are two basic squirrel calls on the market. One is mouth-operated, much like crow and waterfowl calls, and the other is a bellows-type call, which is operated by hand. The slate box call used by turkey hunters can also be used to imitate the call of the squirrel. Some successful hunters even claim that fifty-cent pieces struck edge to edge will produce a reasonable facsimile of a squirrel chuckle.

No matter what type of call is used, the hunter attempts to imitate the familiar bark of the squirrel. While a call may occasionally draw a squirrel within gun or archery range of the hunter, this is rarely the main purpose of calling. The object is to make old bushytail sound off, revealing its location. The hunter can then plan a stalk to get within effective gun or bow range. The fox squirrel is particularly vulnerable to this maneuver, as it loves to chatter.

Squirrel calls are available in most sporting goods stores, and they are listed in many of the outdoor magazines—usually in ads from major game-call manufacturers.

Squirrel calls can be useful in certain hunting situations.

The squirrel call has never played a major role in my own squirrel hunting activities. I suppose it's because I have enjoyed enough success by employing the traditional hunting methods. I much prefer to locate game using my knowledge of its habits. And once I spot a squirrel I like the challenge of stalking it or waiting quietly in a blind until it makes a false move.

The call can be a handy tool, though, particularly in woods new to a hunter, where it helps pinpoint the location of squirrels quickly.

OTHER TACTICS

Team hunting in pairs is also effective at times, with one hunter driving the game toward the other. A simpler form of this method might involve nothing more than flushing game from one side of a tree to the other in order to line up a better shot.

The squirrel's natural curiosity sometimes spells its doom with this method. Team hunters can use this nosiness to make a squirrel move. While one hunter remains on the alert, his partner takes a nail and scratches softly on the bark of a tree in which he knows a squirrel is located. This imitation of a fellow squirrel moving along the tree trunk will usually draw a fatal move. Some hunters use their knives to make acorn-sized hummocks under a tree they know squirrels are hiding in, or they turn stones over so the damp side is facing up. Then they conceal themselves and wait for a bushytail to investigate.

Another exciting and productive method of hunting squirrels is from a boat. The hunter should check the hunting regulations closely before undertaking this method, though, as state laws vary considerably on their treatment of hunting over water. A number of states have restrictions on the use of rifles from boats and some outlaw hunting from outboard-powered boats. In my home state of Virginia, for example, it is unlawful to shoot or carry a loaded rifle over public inland waters.

This, of course, eliminates the use of a .22-caliber rifle. From a practical standpoint this is of little importance, as a rocking or moving boat makes it just about impossible to achieve the accuracy necessary to bag squirrels consistently with a rifle.

Most hunters are familiar with waterfowl regulations that prohibit shooting from a boat powered by an outboard motor. The squirrel hunter can get caught under this rule, too, and you would have a difficult time convincing a warden that you were only out hunting squirrels, particularly if the area contains good duck populations.

Still, this method can be quite effective when squirrels come to the edge of the water to quench their thirst. This often occurs after a feeding period, so the hunter can time his hunting a little later in the day than is customary for prime-time squirrel hunting.

My personal choice for water's edge squirrels is to drift slowly down a woodland stream in a light boat or canoe. I usually combine squirrel hunting with a duck hunt, and on good days I'm able to collect a mixed bag of fat gray squirrels, mallards, and wood ducks. In fact, it was on a duck hunt that I learned about this method of taking squirrels. That first squirrel came as a bonus on a jump-shooting outing.

By necessity, as well as by choice, I use a shotgun for this kind of squirrel hunting. I prefer a drably painted boat and camouflage clothing. This is one of my favorite kinds of hunting. On occasions, I have even carried along a fishing outfit and cast for bass when the hunting was slow.

I have never tried hunting the shorelines of a lake or pond, but some of my friends have done it with excellent results.

Chapter
5

BUSHYTAILS IN YOUR OWN BACKYARD

Of the fifty states that compose our nation, forty-nine report the presence of tree squirrels within their boundaries. Only Hawaii, far out in the Pacific Ocean, is without at least one species of tree squirrel. "We don't have any and don't want any," said a wildlife biologist I talked to on the phone. He obviously hadn't learned to appreciate this fine little game animal.

Only one or two species are found in a few other states, and squirrel hunting is prohibited in several western states. But regardless of where you live in the Lower Forty-Eight you don't have to go far to find some good squirrel hunting. It's interesting that throughout much of America, squirrels—mostly eastern grays, but also some fox squirrels—have turned up in city or suburban parks far beyond their normal range. As alluded to earlier, this was probably the work of some well-intentioned individuals who simply wanted squirrels in their part of the country. In talking to various state wildlife agencies I found this situation in a number of states (e.g., eastern gray squirrels in California).

The following information is based on the results of a survey made specifically for this book. The details were gathered from state game departments, along with interviews with local outdoor writers.

ALABAMA

There are four species of tree squirrels in Alabama: the southern gray squirrel, the Louisiana gray squirrel, the Bachman's fox squirrel, and the southern fox squirrel. All are subspecies of the eastern gray or southern fox squirrel.

According to Walton Lowry of the *Birmingham News*, Alabama hunters sometimes refer to squirrels as "tree rats," but surveys over the years show that squirrel hunting is very popular among Alabama sportsmen. An estimated 25 percent of the approximately 800,000 licensed hunters are avid bushytail hunters. Many of them like to use treeing hounds. "Hunting squirrels with dogs is very popular here," said a spokesman for the Department of Conservation and Natural Resources. "They use all kinds of dogs, treeing hounds as well as little cur dogs that tree by sight."

Squirrel hunting is good to excellent throughout the state in areas where suitable habitat can be found, and the future looks bright in those locales. A trend toward replacing hardwoods with fast-growing pines worries some avid squirrel hunters, but solid hunting opportunities remain.

The hunting season runs from the first of October through February.

Alabama Department of Conservation and Natural Resources
Game and Freshwater Fisheries Division
64 North Union Street, Suite 468
Montgomery, AL 36130–1459
334–242–3467
www.dcnr.state.al.us/agfd

ALASKA

The frisky little red squirrel is one of two tree squirrels found in the forty-ninth state. It isn't hunted in Alaska, or anywhere else in its wide range, as it isn't considered a game animal. There is no open or closed season on the little critter and very little interest in a state best known for its big-game hunting.

There is also a population of northern flying squirrels in the southeast portion of the state. But they are protected here as they are throughout most of their range.

Alaska Department of Fish and Game
Division of Wildlife Conservation
Box 25526
Juneau, AK 99802–5526
907–465–4100
www.adfg.state.ak.us

ARIZONA

Thanks to the handsome little Abert squirrel, Arizona can claim the title of "Squirrel Hunting Capital of the West." The Arizona gray is also hunted, but is not as popular because of its shy and secretive nature. Hunters here often have a hard time locating this tree squirrel. The best Abert hunting is in the Long Valley–Mogollon Rim area of the state.

According to a survey conducted by the Arizona Game and Fish Department a number of years ago, the leading squirrel-producing counties were Coconino, Yavapai, and Gila, but Navajo and Greenlee Counties were also kind to Abert squirrel hunters.

The season on squirrels opens in early October and continues until late November. The hunting is generally good throughout the season, but the ear tufts of the squirrel are fully developed near the end of the season. The mounted Abert squirrel makes a handsome trophy.

The Kaibab squirrel, Huachuca gray of southern Arizona, Apache squirrel, and red squirrel and chickaree are also found in the state, but they are not hunted.

Arizona Game and Fish Department
2221 West Greenway Road
Phoenix, AZ 85023
602–942–3000
www.gf.state.az.us

ARKANSAS

Squirrels rank high on the list of favorite game animals for many avid hunters in the Razorback State. With a fall season running from early September through February in the northern part of the state, one running from early October through February in the southern regions, and a month-long spring season opening in the middle of May, hunters get plenty of opportunities to hunt squirrels here.

The fall hunting is considered best after the leaves have fallen and visibility is much better. The use of dogs is prohibited during the spring season, but they see a lot of action during the long fall and winter season.

Both the eastern gray squirrel and the southern fox squirrel are found in the state. Hunting is good along the creek and river bottoms and in the hardwood forests of the northeastern part of the state. Approximately 70 percent of Arkansas is in timberlands, and the future of squirrel hunting is secure. The only exception to this is in the East Arkansas Delta, where the land is being drained and cleared. Particularly good are the timbered areas of the Ozark and Ouachita Mountains. Outdoor writer John Heuston of Little Rock reports good success in the Twin Lakes Area around Norfolk and Bull Shoals Lakes.

Arkansas Game and Fish Commission
No. 2 Natural Resources Drive
Little Rock, AR 72205
501–223–6300
www.agfc.state.ar.us

CALIFORNIA

The big western gray squirrel is the prize for squirrel hunters in California, though very few hunters bother with squirrels. Most of the squirrel hunting here is done by transplanted eastern or southern hunters who find the big gray squirrel an exciting quarry and delicious table fare. The animal is shy and elusive, however, and a true challenge.

The western gray squirrel is found in the timbered mountains and in the oak woodlands of the foothills and valleys. Some of the best squirrel hunting in California is found in the Cascade and Sierra Nevada Mountain Ranges at elevations of 2,000 to 3,000 feet.

There are isolated populations of fox and eastern gray squirrels in California, but hunters show little interest in them. The chickaree squirrel is present in the state as well, but is not considered a game animal.

The Golden State squirrel season is long, running from the middle of September through January.

California Department of Fish and Game
1416 Ninth Street

Sacramento, CA 95814
916–445–0411
www.dfg.ca.gov

COLORADO

Even in game-rich Colorado squirrel hunting has a few followers. There are a handful of hunters who place it ahead of popular species like elk, mule deer, and other big game. "You don't have to quarter a squirrel," joked one fading big-game hunter who had obviously tired of quartering elk and other big game to pack out.

Of the three squirrels found in the state—the Abert, southern fox squirrel, and red squirrel—only the Abert and the fox are hunted. The Abert and red squirrel are native, but the fox squirrel is believed to have been introduced from neighboring Nebraska.

The fox squirrel was only recently classified as a game animal and given the protection of a closed season. Hunting is usually permitted from October 1 through February. Several years ago, state game biologist Robert J. Tully observed that squirrel hunting is a quality sport that would eventually attract more hunter interest.

The range of the fox squirrel is restricted to the Eastern Slope, with the heaviest populations concentrated along the lower Poudre River and eastward along the South Platte River. It is also found along other streams and ditches on the Eastern Slope where cottonwoods and willows are present, and around Lamar, Rock Ford, and La Junta. Colorado fox squirrels are dependent upon grain for most of their diet, though they do eat nuts and fruits when such delicacies are available.

Management of the fox squirrel is relatively new in Colorado, and its range can probably be expanded by stocking—even onto the Western Slope of the Rocky Mountains.

Colorado Division of Wildlife
6060 Broadway
Denver, CO 80216
303–297–1192
http://wildlife.state.co.us

CONNECTICUT

The gray squirrel, the only game squirrel present in Connecticut, receives somewhat limited attention from hunters in this New England state, and large numbers of grays go unharvested every season. Squirrels are particularly abundant in the mixed hardwood forests of the northeastern and northwestern sections of the state. As the stands of hardwood continue to age, squirrel hunting should improve—more acorns and other nuts and more aging oaks for den trees.

In an effort to encourage squirrel hunting, a number of years ago wildlife managers of the Department of Environmental Protection extended the hunting season to three segments running from early September through February. Many hunters consider early November, just after the leaves have fallen, to be the most productive time to hunt bushytails.

The chief of the game division pointed out that there is a preponderance of oak in Connecticut, and he felt that acorns are the single most important food in the squirrel's diet during those cold New England winters.

Connecticut Department of Environmental Protection
Wildlife Division
79 Elm Street
Hartford, CT 06106–5127
860–424–3011
http://dep.state.ct.us

DELAWARE

The gray squirrel is a popular game animal in this little state on the Atlantic coast. While still reasonably abundant, the squirrel has suffered from the loss of habitat here. Agricultural practices and an expanding human population always in need of housing have eliminated much of what were once vast forests of hardwoods where the animals flourished.

But good squirrel hunting is still available. A long fall season opens in the middle of September and runs in segments through the middle of January.

Delaware Department of Natural Resources and
    Environmental Control
Division of Fish and Wildlife
89 Kings Highway
Dover, DE 19901
302–739–5297
www.dnrec.state.de.us

FLORIDA

Both fox and gray squirrels are native to Florida, and the state's outdoor-loving sportsmen prize their squirrel hunting. Florida is one of the few states that over the years has had separate bag limits on its two species of squirrels.

Florida hunters spend more time and effort in harvesting squirrels than they do in any other kind of hunting, including deer, quail, or turkey. Placed in a line—nose to tail—a single season's harvest of the frisky little animals would stretch from Waycross, Georgia, to Miami, Florida, a distance of 420 miles. One authority estimated the state's squirrel population at 4,287,000 animals.

The best hunting areas are located in north and central Florida, with the gray preferring hardwood hammocks. The fox likes the Florida piney woods, where pine seeds are its favorite food.

The squirrel seasons in Florida vary slightly between zones, but generally squirrel hunting is legal from the middle of November into early March. Charley Waterman, a well-known Florida outdoor writer, considers December and January the best months to hunt bushytails.

Florida Game and Freshwater Fish Commission
620 South Meridian Street
Tallahassee, FL 32399–1600
850–488–4676
http://myfwc.com

GEORGIA

Just like the rest of the Southeast, squirrel hunting ranks high among the pursuits of Georgia hunters. Squirrel hunting is generally good all over the Cracker State, and both the gray squirrel and the larger fox squirrel get attention from the state's avid hunting population.

While hunting is generally good statewide, it might be best in the northern part of the state where there is more timber. But it can be just as good in central Georgia and some sections in the south. Georgia, like most southeastern states, is losing much of its hardwood forests to fast-growing pines, and that has had a deterrent effect on squirrel hunting, but good hunting territory is still widely available.

The Georgia season is a long one, giving hunters ample opportunity to hunt the solid population of squirrels. It opens in the middle of August and runs through February.

Hunting is good throughout the season, though chiggers, ticks, and other insects may be a problem early in the season. The first frost usually eliminates them.

Georgia Department of Natural Resources
Wildlife Resources Division
2070 US Highway 78 Southeast
Social Circle, GA 30025
770–918–6416
www.gadnr.org

IDAHO

Rich in big game and a wide variety of game birds, Idaho has no native squirrels except the little pine squirrel, which is completely protected. There is no open hunting season on the little squirrel and no interest among hunters. The general feeling seems to be that the animal is of more value from an aesthetic standpoint. "We do have some fox squirrels and eastern gray squirrels in a number of suburban areas such as city parks," said a wildlife manager with the Department of Fish and Game. "They are not considered game animals here and so can be hunted, but interested hunters should check with local authorities. About firing a gun in a suburban area, for example."

These animals were apparently introduced by private citizens. Many are of the "peanut fed" variety. From a hunting point of view, you can mark Idaho off for squirrels.

Idaho Department of Fish and Game
600 South Walnut Street
P.O. Box 25
Boise, ID 83707
1–800–635–7820, 208–334–3700
www.fishandgame.idaho.gov

ILLINOIS

For a number of years, Illinois hunters bagged more squirrels than cottontail rabbits, once the generally accepted number-one game animal in America. A few years ago the annual harvest of squirrels was in the range of two to three million, with about half the state's licensed sportsmen hunting bushytails. There has been a decline in squirrel hunting participation in recent years, according to a spokesman for the Division of Wildlife Resources. "The average bag remains high, but squirrels have had to yield hunting time to deer and turkeys." Today the annual harvest is just under a million animals. Despite that, squirrel hunting in the state remains excellent.

Both fox and gray squirrels are found in Illinois, with two subspecies of the gray present. *Sciurus carolinensis pennsylvanicus* lives in the northern two-thirds of the state, and *S. c. carolinensis* in the remaining third. Fox squirrels are found statewide, but are probably more abundant in the southern portion of the state.

An albino form of the gray squirrel lives in the city of Olney. The estimated population of these little squirrels ranges around a thousand animals. There is also a melanistic (nearly black) shade of gray in the vicinity of Rock Island on the Mississippi River.

Some of the best hunting areas include the Shawnee National Forest in southern Illinois, the heavily timbered creek bottoms in the south, the Mississippi and Illinois River valleys, and the valleys of other major streams.

In many parts of Illinois large corporations are buying up bottomlands, removing the timber, and planting soybeans. This practice is a major threat to squirrel hunting. On the other hand, in the Shawnee National Forest the squirrel's future looks bright.

The squirrel season opens in early August in southern Illinois, but not until a month later in the north. Both seasons run until the middle of November. August and September are considered prime hunting month, as squirrels are busy harvesting and feeding in the hickory groves during that period.

Illinois Department of Natural Resources
Division of Wildlife Resources
Lincoln Tower Plaza
524 South Second Street
Springfield, IL 62701–1787
217–782–6384
http://dnr.state.il.us

INDIANA

Squirrel hunting is popular in Indiana, and hunters make a healthy harvest each autumn. The big fox squirrel makes up approximately two-thirds of the total take, with grays filling the rest of the bag. Timber removal from much of the Hoosier National Forest once threatened the forest-loving gray squirrel, but it's no longer a problem. The harvest of timber has declined in recent years. Both the fox and gray are most abundant in the southern part of the state. The gray makes its best showing in the south-central hills, where its population density is about equal to that of the fox squirrel.

Indiana's squirrel season occurs at a time of year when there is little other hunting available, which may account for some of the strong interest from hunters. The season runs from mid-August to mid-October.

Indiana Department of Natural Resources
Division of Fish and Wildlife
402 West Washington Street
Room W273
Indianapolis, IN 46204
317–232–4080
www.state.in.us/dnr

IOWA

With good populations of fox and gray squirrels, Iowa can afford to have a long hunting season open—early September through January. While Iowa hunters prize their abundant squirrel numbers, the animals are actually underharvested in this state noted for its corn crops. Obviously, the little bushytails find plenty of ripe corn to feed on when the season opens in September. The hunting is good when squirrels are raiding ripe corn and cutting ripe nuts, but most sportsmen consider late fall, when the leaves have fallen, the prime time to hunt squirrels. They are, of course, more visible in the woods at that time.

Eastern and southeastern Iowa are the best areas for gray squirrels, while the big fox squirrel is present statewide.

The Iowa Conservation Commission has been committed to a program of land acquisition to protect timber, and state foresters refrain from cutting den trees. So the outlook for squirrel hunting in the state is good.

Iowa Department of Natural Resources
502 East Ninth Street
Des Moines, IA 50319
515–281–5145
www.iowadnr.com

KANSAS

A few years ago the annual bag of squirrels in Kansas ran between 300,000 and 400,000 animals. The big plains state has both fox and gray squirrels, but the larger fox squirrel is the more abundant of the two species.

The timbered eastern half of the state offers the best hunting, but scattered stands of timber in the west near the Colorado border are also good. The Kansas squirrel season is one of the longest in the nation, opening in early June and running through January. October through December are considered the best hunting months.

The healthy squirrel population has benefited from the management of other game species such as deer, turkeys, pheasants, quail, and waterfowl. The future of squirrel hunting is promising in Kansas.

Kansas Department of Wildlife and Parks
512 Southeast 25th Avenue
Pratt, KS 67124
620–672–5911
www.kdwp.state.ks.us

KENTUCKY

The gray squirrel tops the list of small-game animals in the Bluegrass State, except for those years in which an abundance of cottontail rabbits creates a boon for hunters. Kentucky hunters bag mostly gray squirrels. The fox squirrel makes up only around 10 percent of the total squirrel bag.

The gray is found in all of the state's 120 counties, but is most abundant in the wooded areas of eastern, southeastern, and western Kentucky. The highest number of fox squirrels can be found in the central Bluegrass region and in the bottom areas along the Mississippi and Ohio Rivers in the western part of the state.

Cooperation between state biologists and foresters has stimulated the growth of mast-producing trees, creating a bright future for the squirrel hunter here. The squirrel season is split in Kentucky. The first season is brief, running for two weeks in early June, and the second one opens in the middle of August and runs through January. September is considered the top hunting month.

Kentucky Department of Fish and Wildlife
1 Game Farm Road
Frankfort, KY 40601
1–800–858–1549
http://fw.ky.gov

LOUISIANA

The squirrel is the most heavily hunted small-game animal in Louisiana. Three subspecies of fox squirrels (big-headed, delta, and Bachman's) and two subspecies of the gray squirrel (bayou and southern) keep Louisiana squirrel hunting varied and interesting.

In the hilly sections of the state the best squirrel hunting is found along stream borders. Veteran hunters also like the pin oak flats and oak ridges. Stands of beech trees are good when the mast crop is present, although acorns are the single most important squirrel food in the Bayou State.

Since 1961 the Louisiana Wildlife and Fisheries Commission has been conducting squirrel studies on the Thistlewaite Game Management Area, a 10,000-acre hardwood forest located in St. Landry Parish. This project has since been completed, and much valuable information gained regarding squirrel management.

The squirrel-hunting season in Louisiana usually runs from early October to the middle of February.

Louisiana Department of Wildlife and Fisheries
P.O. Box 98000
Baton Rouge, LA 70898–9000
225–765–2346
www.wlf.state.la.us

MAINE

Although Maine has long been one of the East's top hunting states, interest in squirrel hunting remains low, with the exception of a few dedicated small-game hunters. The eastern gray squirrel and the little pine squirrel make up the state's squirrel population.

Gray squirrels are reasonably abundant, although their range is limited to the mixed forests of the southern part of the Pine Tree State. The little red squirrel, which isn't considered a game animal, is found in the north.

Old-time Maine hunters still speak of witnessing mass squirrel migrations. Large numbers of bushytails evidently swam rivers and lakes and moved rapidly through the forests, possibly to escape Maine's bitter winter weather.

The Maine squirrel season opens in early October and continues through December, well after the leaves have dropped.

Maine Department of Inland Fisheries and Wildlife
284 State Street
State House Station 41
Augusta, ME 04333–0041
207–287–8000
www.state.me.us/iwf

MARYLAND

The late Don Carpenter, an outdoor writer based in Annapolis, considered the squirrel the number-one game animal in the Old Line State in his day. Both the fox and gray squirrel are present, though the fox squirrel population is very small due to the loss of chestnut trees.

Squirrels are found throughout the state, but the best hunting is usually in the four mountainous western counties and the nine agricultural counties on the Eastern Shore. The squirrel season usually runs from early October through January.

Maryland Department of Natural Resources
Wildlife and Heritage Division
Tawes State Office Building, E-1
580 Taylor Avenue
Annapolis, MD 21401
410–260–8540
ww.dnr.state.md.us

MASSACHUSETTS

A few years ago state wildlife biologists ranked the squirrel fourth in the Bay State, behind pheasant, grouse, and rabbits. However, based on hunter success the squirrel came in first, as 72 percent of all squirrel hunters brought something home.

The gray is the only squirrel found in Massachusetts. Forests here are maturing more rapidly than they are being cut, and the future of squirrel hunting looks promising. Hunting is generally good statewide.

The squirrel season usually opens in early September in the western zone and in late October in the eastern zone. Both seasons close in early January.

Massachusetts Division of Fisheries and Wildlife
Field Headquarters
One Rabbit Hill Road
Westboro, MA 01581
508–792–7270
www.mass.gov/dfwele/dpt_toc.htm

MICHIGAN

Michigan small-game hunters enjoy targeting both fox and gray squirrels. Over the years the fox squirrel has received particularly heavy hunting in the Lower Peninsula. These squirrels are found throughout the southern part of Michigan, particularly in lands associated with agriculture. A few are present in the Upper Peninsula, but they are completely protected in that part of the state.

Gray squirrels show up statewide, but are most abundant in the forested northern part of the state. The black phase of the gray squirrel was once fairly common, and it was completely protected for a time.

Wildlife managers predict a rosy future for the abundant fox squirrel, but less of one for the gray squirrels. The Michigan squirrel season opens in the middle of September and runs through December.

Michigan Wildlife Division
Department of Natural Resources
Box 30444
Lansing, MI 48909
517–373–1263
www.michigan.gov/dnr

MINNESOTA

Minnesota hunters typically bag half a million squirrels annually. Gray squirrels make the major contribution to that harvest, but the fox squirrel kill is also strong. Hunting is obviously good for these species. Though reasonably abundant, the red squirrel is not considered a game animal.

The largest numbers come from southeastern Minnesota, but the Minnesota and Mississippi River basins are also productive. Hardwood forests in east-central Minnesota are popular hunting areas, as are scattered woodlots in the prairie region of the state. Jack Connor, longtime Minneapolis outdoor writer, considered the counties of Anoka, Isanti, and Sherburne north and west of Minneapolis–St. Paul his favorite squirrel hunting territory.

The future of squirrel hunting in Minnesota looks promising because of the abundance of natural habitat. Nuts and acorns make up the bulk of the Minnesota bushytail's diet, but corn is also an important ingredient when available.

The Minnesota squirrel-hunting season opens in the middle of September and continues through February. Controlling the abundant squirrel population has been a major management problem in Minnesota. When numbers rise dramatically the squirrels damage crops and strip the bark from valuable maple trees.

Minnesota Department of Natural Resources
Division of Fish and Wildlife
Box 7 DNR Building
500 Lafayette
St. Paul, MN 55155
651–296–6157
www.dnr.state.mn.us

MISSISSIPPI

Gray squirrels are the most widely distributed game species in Mississippi, and over the years there have been more hunters afield after gray and fox squirrels than in pursuit of any other game. That may be changing slightly with the rapid growth of deer and turkey populations, as both of these species are very popular with Deep South hunters.

The Mississippi gray, commonly called the cat squirrel here, is somewhat smaller than grays in the Ozarks and farther north. The black phase of the gray is fairly common in the state.

There are two recognized subspecies of the fox squirrel in Mississippi. One is known locally as the hill fox squirrel and the other as the delta fox squirrel. The range of the latter is limited to the Yazoo–Mississippi Delta, but the hill fox lives in suitable habitat throughout the state.

Squirrel hunting is generally good all over Mississippi, but the best hunting can probably be found in the bayou swamps and the forests of the Delta. Gray squirrels like stream and creek bottoms and swamps supporting oak, hickory, gum, magnolia, beech, and other nut-bearing trees. On hills and slopes they prefer mixed stands of timber.

The squirrel season opens in early October and continues to late December.

Mississippi Department of Wildlife, Fisheries, and Parks
1505 Eastover Drive
Jackson, MS 39211
601–432–2400
www.mdwfp.com

MISSOURI

With fox and gray squirrels abundant in Mark Twain's state, Missouri squirrel hunters bag in excess of a million squirrels annually. The harvest of fox squirrels slightly exceeds the gray bag in a typical year, but often it is a neck-and-neck race. Squirrel hunting is considered good to excellent statewide, though some hunters consider the famous Ozark Hills and the Missouri River bottomlands among the best areas to target. Creek bottoms are good throughout the state. Many small woodlots in the prairie country of western and northern Missouri have thriving populations of squirrels.

IN THE SQUIRREL WOODS

Squirrel hunting is a tradition that each generation passes down to the next.

Despite their diminutive size, squirrels remain one of the most sought-after game animals in North America. (Monte Burch)

Scopes that gather light are very useful in the squirrel woods, where shadows often linger throughout the day. (Monte Burch)

A stand can be as simple as a seat on the ground beside a tree, although it pays to scout well before the hunt to make sure squirrels are in the area. (Monte Burch)

Gray (above) and fox squirrels make up the bulk of the annual hunter harvest. (Monte Burch)

All squirrels take advantage of the variety of hard mast produced in mature hardwood forests. (Monte Burch)

Fox squirrels can wreak havoc on domestic crops like corn. Farmers in such areas are often happy to allow hunters on their land to help control the population. (Monte Burch)

Many novice hunters get their start in the squirrel woods. This youngster is admiring a fox squirrel. (Monte Burch)

The author takes an impromptu stand while waiting for some late-morning action.

Smart hunters know the value of setting up near squirrel dens such as this one. (Monte Burch)

A variety of squirrel calls can help the hunter locate hidden animals, particularly in new areas. (Monte Burch)

Scouting is important no matter what type of hunting you're doing. Here, the author is studying the ground beneath a nut tree for signs of recent activity.

In good habitat, it's often possible to take several squirrels from a single stand.

Camping in the woods allows hunters to get out right at first light, when squirrel movement is usually at its peak. (Monte Burch)

Squirrels spend quite a bit of time on the ground, but most shot opportunities still come from above. (Monte Burch)

Spotting a squirrel in dense woodlands before the leaves are down takes a sharp, experienced eye. (Monte Burch)

Although many squirrel hunters go afield with scoped .22 rifles, hunting with a small-caliber muzzleloader offers some interesting challenges. (Monte Burch)

The fox is more widely distributed than the gray, but the latter is more abundant in the Ozarks and Mississippi Lowland regions. Modern timber management on over two million acres of state and federal land assures the future of squirrel hunting, a popular pastime here.

Missouri has long been noted for its extended squirrel season, with hunting allowed from late May through the middle of January. The first two weeks of the season and late summer through October are considered prime hunting periods.

Missouri Department of Conservation
P.O. Box 180
Jefferson City, MO 65102–0180
573–751–4115
www.mdc.mo.gov

MONTANA

The fox squirrel is the only game squirrel found in Big Sky Country. The range of the fox is limited to eastern Montana, and it mostly lives along the Missouri and Yellowstone River bottoms. The little red squirrel is found throughout the national forests here.

Squirrels are not classified as game animals in Montana, and very few sportsmen hunt them. There are no closed seasons and no hunting regulations. "Most of the squirrels live in city parks," joked a spokesman for the state wildlife agency.

Montana Fish, Wildlife, and Parks
1420 East Sixth Avenue
P.O. Box 200701
Helena, MT 59620–0701
406–444–2535
www.fwp.state.mt.us

NEBRASKA

Nebraska hunters bag several hundred squirrels each year, most of which are fox squirrels. There are few, if any, gray squirrels in Nebraska. While those who participate in the sport find it rewarding, most hunters here do not pursue squirrels. Counties in southeastern and northeastern Nebraska are the best bets for squirrel hunting. Since Nebraska is an agricultural state, the fox squirrels feed heavily on corn.

The squirrel season is a long one, opening in early August and running through most of January. November is perhaps the best month for hunting squirrels in Nebraska.

Nebraska Game and Parks Commission
2200 North 33rd Street
Lincoln, NE 68503
402–471–0641
www.ngpc.state.ne.us

NEVADA

The only squirrels present in Nevada are Douglas and flying squirrels, which aren't hunted. Nevada has never had an open season on squirrels and does not anticipate one in the future.

Nevada Division of Wildlife
P.O. Box 10678
Reno, NV 89520
775–688–1500
http://dcnr.nv.gov

NEW HAMPSHIRE

The gray squirrel is the only species present in huntable numbers in New Hampshire, though there are populations of the little pine, or red, squirrel. Over the years interest in squirrel hunting has been low, with deer, grouse, turkeys, and woodcock attracting most of the hunting attention. In recent years, however, there has been an increased interest in hunting squirrels.

The gray squirrel population is found primarily in the southern part of New Hampshire, south of the White Mountains. The season on grays usually opens in early October and runs through December.

New Hampshire Fish and Game Department
11 Hazen Drive
Concord, NH 03301
603–271–3211
http://wildlife.state.nh.us

NEW JERSEY

At one time the squirrel was second only to the cottontail rabbit in popularity in the Garden State, but growing deer and turkey populations have changed that. Still, squirrel hunting garners its share of interest. The gray is the only squirrel found here, but the black phase of the species is present throughout the state.

The best squirrel hunting can be had in hardwood stands of timber in the northern part of New Jersey. Squirrels are so abundant in certain regions that the Division of Fish, Game, and Wildlife published a paper a number of years ago advising homeowners on how to deal with them.

With a split season—the first open from late September to early December and the second open from mid-December through much of February—there are plenty of opportunities for the New Jersey squirrel hunter.

New Jersey Department of Environmental Protection
Division of Fish, Game, and Wildlife

P.O. Box 400
Trenton, NJ 08625–0400
609–292–2965
www.state.nj.us/dep/fgw

NEW MEXICO

The Abert and Arizona gray are the only squirrels present in New Mexico. The Arizona gray has been completely protected for a number of years (no hunting allowed). The season on the Abert is very brief, lasting just a week or so in September. Obviously, squirrel hunting is very limited in New Mexico and few hunters pursue it.

The Abert is found as far south as the Mimbres Mountains southeast of Silver City. Its range runs north through the Mogollons and the Black Range into the Frisco Mountains, the Datils, the San Mateos, and the Magdalenas. In the north, the Abert is found in the Sandias, Mansanos, Sangre de Cristos, San Juans, Jemez, Mt. Taylor, and Zuni Mountains. It is also found in the Chuska Mountains.

Like most squirrels, the Abert buries a lot of nuts and is credited with reforesting much of what is now New Mexico. The area is thought to have been swept clear of timber by glaciers during the Ice Age.

New Mexico Department of Game and Fish
P.O. Box 25112
Santa Fe, NM 87504–5112
1–800–862–9310
www.wildlife.state.nm.us

NEW YORK

Squirrel hunters will find both fox and gray squirrels in New York, but the range of the former is somewhat limited. This big squirrel is fairly common in Chatauqua County, and sightings have been reported in Otsego County. But the gray squirrel gets most of the hunting attention here. It is often referred to as the gray bannertail or black or cat squirrel. It is found throughout New York but shuns the higher elevations in the Adirondacks and Catskills. Back at the turn of the century the black phase of the gray was actually more common than the gray phase, but not so today.

The New York squirrel season is a long one, opening in early September and running through February. Hunting is usually best during the early weeks of the season.

New York Department of Environmental Conservation
Fish and Wildlife Division
50 Wolf Road
Albany, NY 12233
518-457-5400
www.dec.state.ny.us

NORTH CAROLINA

The gray squirrel is the official state mammal of North Carolina. While both the gray and fox squirrel suffered from heavy logging here early in the last century, better forest management has created a brighter picture, and there has been a slight increase in the overall squirrel population in the Tar Heel State. The fox and gray are both popular among North Carolina hunters.

The prime hunting areas are along the streams of the Coastal Plain, in the hardwoods of the Piedmont region, and in the mountains where hardwoods thrive. The range of the fox squirrel is limited to the Sandhills and lower Coastal Plain woodlands.

The season on the more abundant gray squirrel opens in the middle of October and runs through January. The fox squirrel season opens concurrently with the gray season and runs through December.

North Carolina Wildlife Resources Commission
512 North Salisbury Street
Raleigh, NC 27604–1188
919–662–4370
http://216.27.49.98

NORTH DAKOTA

Fox and eastern gray squirrels are present in North Dakota. The gray is a native species, but the fox is believed to have entered the state from Minnesota or South Dakota. Very few hunters go after squirrels here, but there may be an increasing hunting interest in the Red River Valley, where very few other small-game animals are found.

The best hunting areas are the Turtle Mountains, Pembian Hills, and the wooded river valleys of the Cheyenne, James, and Missouri Rivers. The hunting season for squirrels opens in the middle of September and runs through December.

North Dakota Game and Fish Department
100 North Bismarck Expressway
Bismarck, ND 58501
701–328–6300
www.state.nd.us/gnf

OHIO

In terms of hunter interest, squirrels are the most important forest game in Ohio. Over half of the hunters in the Buckeye State pursue the fox or gray squirrel. The fox makes its best showing in the woodlot country of western and northeastern Ohio, while the gray squirrel does best in the unglaciated, hilly forests in the southeastern and south-central portions of the state. The best squirrel hunting is found in the southeastern hills.

Back in 1957 the squirrel season was doubled from twenty-six to fifty-two days, and studies since then have shown that the more liberal season has had no deleterious effect on squirrel populations. Some hunters prefer early September when the squirrels are actively cutting nuts, while others like October and November when the weather is cooler. Many consider the best hunting time to be mid-September through October.

The Ohio squirrel-hunting season runs from the middle of August through January. Wildlife managers have made it clear that as long as squirrel populations remain stable the liberal season will continue.

Ohio Department of Natural Resources
Division of Wildlife
1840 Belcher Drive
Columbus, OH 43224–1329
614–265–6300
www.dnr.state.oh.us

OKLAHOMA

Both the fox and gray squirrel are present in the Sooner State, and with a season that runs from the middle of May through January, Oklahoma hunters have ample time to enjoy one of their favorite kinds of hunting. The spring and fall months are considered prime for squirrel hunting.

The best hunting is found in eastern Oklahoma, with the Deep Fork of the Red River and the extreme southeastern part of the state considered a great area. "Lots of acorns in that area and pecans are coming on. Squirrels, of course, love them," notes Thayne Smith, veteran Oklahoma outdoor writer.

Oklahoma Department of Wildlife Conservation
1801 North Lincoln Street
Oklahoma City, OK 73105
405–521–3851
www.wildlifedepartment.com

OREGON

The western gray squirrel, often called the silver gray squirrel in Oregon, is the only huntable squirrel in this Pacific coast state. Few Oregon nimrods bother to hunt squirrels, though, as the western gray squirrel becomes elusive and very shy of human beings when pressured.

The best hunting areas are west of the Cascade Mountains, in the oak and fir forests or around the nut-growing agricultural areas. Oak groves on the east side of Mount Hood also contain good gray squirrel populations. A few eastern grays, all imports, are found in city parks.

Squirrel hunting is permitted year-round in northwest Oregon, but is limited to a two-month autumn season in southwest Oregon and the Hood River area.

Oregon Department of Fish and Wildlife
P.O. Box 59
Salem, OR 97308
503–949–6020
www.dfw.state.or.us

PENNSYLVANIA

Both the fox and gray squirrel inhabit Pennsylvania, with the gray present in good numbers wherever it can find suitable habitat. The big fox squirrel usually avoids Pennsylvania's rugged mountains, preferring small park-like woodlots in the western and southern parts of the state. Little red squirrels are also found here, but they aren't hunted to any degree—if at all.

In addition to the typical gray squirrel, the black phase of the gray is also scattered throughout the state. In some instances, it appears almost jet-black. The pelage of the Pennsylvania fox squirrel ranges from a salt-and-pepper gray to pale gray.

November is the squirrel-hunting month in the Quaker State.

Pennsylvania Game Commission
2001 Elmerton Avenue
Harrisburg, PA 17110–9797
717–787–4250
www.dcnr.state.pa.us

RHODE ISLAND

The gray squirrel is a popular game animal in tiny Rhode Island, particularly among southerners stationed at Rhode Island naval bases. The annual bag is small, maybe a thousand or so bushytails, but when you consider the size of the state and its dense population, the harvest seems pretty respectable.

The gray squirrel occurs throughout Rhode Island, but the best hunting is in the river bottoms and larger swamps. It is the only game squirrel found in the state.

The squirrel-hunting season opens in the middle of October and runs through February. It is put on hold, however, during the shotgun deer season.

Rhode Island Department of Environmental Management
Division of Fish and Wildlife
235 Promenade Street
Providence, RI 02892
401–222–6800
www.state.ri.us/dem

SOUTH CAROLINA

South Carolina hosts fox and gray squirrels, but the fox is not as widespread as the gray. More people hunt squirrels than any other small game in South Carolina, and the state has a large squirrel population.

The mountain counties and the bottomland hardwoods of the Coastal Plain are excellent choices for squirrel hunting. Unfortunately, much of the Coastal Plain is being cleared of hardwoods in favor of fast-growing pines, which represent a serious threat to the squirrel population.

October is a favorite squirrel-hunting month, although the season is a long one. It usually opens in early October and runs through February. Local squirrel hunters often seek out wooded areas adjoining cultivated farmlands.

South Carolina Department of Natural Resources
P.O. Box 167
Columbia, SC 29202
803–734–3886
www.dnr.state.sc.us

SOUTH DAKOTA

The fox squirrel is by far the most common tree squirrel in South Dakota, and it's found everywhere there is suitable habitat. It likes a few trees and a close source of food, such as acorns, corn, or tree buds. The western gray squirrel is found in limited populations in the western part of South Dakota.

For many years the squirrels were unprotected here, with no closed season. But today hunter interest in squirrels is slowly growing. The season opens in early September and runs through most of February.

South Dakota Department of Game, Fish, and Parks
Information Services
523 East Capitol
Pierre, SD 57501
605–773–3485
www.sdgfp.info/Index.htm

TENNESSEE

Fox and gray squirrels are among the most popular small-game animals in the Volunteer State. Grays thrive in most timbered areas throughout the state, but the range of the fox squirrel is generally limited to an area extending from the Knoxville region west to the border.

The loss of bottomland hardwoods and den trees is a major threat to the future of squirrel hunting in Tennessee. Generally, though, the bushytail has a promising future here.

There are two squirrel-hunting seasons in Tennessee. The spring season opens in mid-May and runs for a month. The fall and winter season opens in late August and continues through February. Autumn, after the leaves have fallen from the hardwoods, is a favorite hunting time.

Tennessee Wildlife Resources Agency
P.O. Box 40747
Nashville, TN 37204
615–781–6610
www.state.tn.us/twra

TEXAS

The gray, or cat, squirrel is the most important small-game animal in Texas, although its range is limited to the extreme eastern part of the state. The fox squirrel, on the other hand, is more widespread. Its range extends into the eastern section of the Panhandle and into western Texas along the Rio Grande. Texas hunters typically take over a million squirrels annually, though in recent years an abundant white-tailed deer population has accounted for most of the hunting attention.

In Texas, the gray squirrel lives mainly in dense hammocks of live and water oak, and in deep swamps of cypress, black gum, and magnolia. The gray squirrel is not abundant in the upland forests of Texas, as it is in many parts of its overall range.

The fox squirrel is adaptable to a wide variety of forest habitats, but in most parts of Texas the heaviest populations are found in open upland forests of mixed trees. The ideal habitat is mature oak and hickory woodland broken into small, irregularly shaped tracts of five to twenty acres.

Destruction of habitat and overhunting have been harmful to squirrel populations here over the years. Old records show where a party of four hunters once killed more than a hundred squirrels in a single day in the Big Thicket area of Texas. A few counties still permit year-round hunting for squirrels, and some don't even bother to impose bag limits.

Seasons vary in Texas, with some counties offering spring hunting during the month of May. Many counties offer a fall season that opens in early October and runs through the middle of January. Both spring and fall hunts are popular in Texas.

Texas Parks and Wildlife Department
4200 Smith School Road
Austin, TX 78744
1–800–792–1112
www.tpwd.state.tx.us

UTAH

With only red and flying squirrels present in the mountainous areas of Utah, there is no squirrel-hunting interest in the state. Squirrels are unprotected, but no one hunts them here.

Utah Division of Wildlife Resources
1594 West North Temple
Salt Lake City, UT 84114–6301
801–538–4700
www.nr.utah.gov

VERMONT

Gray squirrels are very abundant in Vermont, and local hunters are showing an increasing interest in them. The best hunting is found in the southeastern and southwestern portions of the state, though squirrels occur statewide where habitat is suitable.

The gray population is healthy and growing in Vermont, and the future looks good for hunters who want to take advantage of it.

The squirrel season opens in early September and continues through December. October is generally considered the top squirrel-hunting month.

Vermont Agency of Natural Resources
Fish and Wildlife Department
103 South Main Street
Waterbury, VT 05671–0501
802–241–3700
www.anr.state.vt.us

VIRGINIA

Squirrel hunting has a long tradition in Virginia, dating back to the first European settlements. Both fox and gray squirrels are found here, but the gray is the predominant species from the tidal area to the Allegheny Mountains. Fox squirrels are found primarily in the western part of the state.

For years, Virginia wildlife managers were plagued by a conglomeration of county seasons set by the General Assembly. Now the season is statewide, running from early September through January.

Millions of acres of forestland in the Jefferson and George Washington National Forests provide ample opportunity for squirrel hunting, but when the mast crop is light the farm woodlots of the Piedmont region are probably better choices.

Virginia is giving attention to its squirrel populations, and barring the senseless destruction of hardwoods for pine tree production, the future of squirrel hunting looks bright.

Virginia Department of Game and Inland Fisheries
4010 West Broad Street
Richmond, VA 23230–1104
434–367–1000
www.dgif.state.va.us

WASHINGTON

While the big western gray squirrel is present in Washington, along with the smaller red and chickaree squirrels, there is no open season on squirrels in this Pacific Northwest state. Squirrels aren't considered game animals, and the western gray is listed as an endangered species. There is plenty of good hunting here, but not for squirrels.

Washington Department of Fish and Wildlife
600 Capitol Way North
Olympia, WA 98501
360–902–2200
http://wdfw.wa.gov

WEST VIRGINIA

West Virginia could well be the most popular squirrel-hunting state in America. For years the gray squirrel was the number-one game animal here, but the growth of the deer and turkey populations has probably robbed it of that ranking. Both the fox and gray squirrel are found in West Virginia, but the gray is by far the most abundant, and, consequently, the most popular among hunters.

Good squirrel hunting can be found throughout the state, except on the high ridges where hemlock and northern hardwood forests predominate. Gray squirrels are scarce at elevations in excess of 3,000 feet, though the little red squirrel likes this kind of habitat. Wildlife managers expect good squirrel hunting to continue almost indefinitely, although a major deterrent would be the loss or destruction of hardwood forests.

The West Virginia squirrel season opens in early October and continues through January. October and November are considered the best hunting months. A few years ago an experimental September season established that squirrel hunting can be good at that time as well, but as of yet wildlife managers have not agreed to continue that early season.

West Virginia Division of Natural Resources
Wildlife Resources Section
State Capitol Complex, Building 3
1900 Kanawha Boulevard
Charleston, WV 25303
304-558-2771
www.wvdnr.gov

WISCONSIN

The fox and gray squirrel are common in Wisconsin, and both are native species. Squirrel hunting is good throughout the state where there is suitable habitat. Many of the state's public hunting grounds are productive, and the future of squirrel hunting in Wisconsin is favorable.

The hunting season runs from the middle of September through January, but the best hunting usually occurs in late October after the leaves have fallen.

Wisconsin Bureau of Wildlife Management
P.O. Box 7921
Madison, WI 53707
608–266–2621
www.dnr.state.wi.us

WYOMING

Wyoming offers fox and gray squirrels, along with reds, but for years they weren't hunted. They weren't even considered game animals, so no hunting regulations applied. But that has changed. Now there are two squirrel seasons, one opening in early September and continuing through December and a second from early January through February.

Wyoming Game and Fish Department
5400 Bishop Boulevard
Cheyenne, WY 82006
307–777–4600
http://gf.state.wy.us

Chapter

6

THE RIFLEMAN'S SMALL GAME

Despite the squirrel's elusive nature, the difficult target it presents, and its fine taste on the table, many hunters dismiss it as unworthy of their attention. They admit that the bushytail is excellent game for young hunters to train on, but for some reason they seem to feel that squirrel hunting is beneath their dignity once they've moved on to larger game.

Admittedly, a squirrel perched nonchalantly in the crotch of a hickory tree is not much of a challenge for a shotgunner at close range, but try swinging on it as it scampers through the swaying branches of a tall oak. Or try to nail it as it races wildly over the leaf-littered floor of a thick forest. The bowhunter will swap a quiver full of blunt-tipped arrows for every bite of tasty meat he puts in the pot, but many archers enjoy the challenge.

But for the best in squirrel hunting, you must go after the little critter with a .22-caliber rifle. For a lot of hunters there is no finer sport than bagging a mess of squirrels with the little .22. Success demands crack shooting, but it can come quickly if you have a sharp eye. And keeping your shooting skills finely honed

A father and son examine a squirrel brought down with a fine rifle shot.

on squirrels will help you come deer season.

One advantage the rifleman has over the shotgunner is the subdued report of the small-caliber rifle. While the bark of a scattergun will send game scurrying, the mild report of a little .22 doesn't seem to alarm squirrels—even those shot at and missed. The report evidently resembles familiar woods noises such as cracking tree branches, a storm, or the snap of a twig when a large animal steps on it. I have often shot at a squirrel, missed, bolted another round into the chamber, and fired again while the squirrel did nothing more than perk up, pause, look around, and then resume cracking and munching an acorn or hickory nut. If you locate a particularly good feeding tree you may be able to bag your limit without moving a single step.

The rifleman also has an advantage when working extremely tall timber where there are few hollow trees and dens. Squirrels resting or feeding high in the treetops in areas like this seem to feel that the height protects them, and they are easier to locate. This is long-range shooting, usually beyond the limited killing range of most shotguns. Success comes only with a good rifle and careful shooting.

A perfect shot for a hunter with a .22-caliber rifle.

The squirrel is the rifleman's small game, and one of the few North American game animals truly appropriate for the small-bore rifle. Of the various hunting tactics discussed earlier, the blind or stand method is by far the best for the rifleman. It gives him time to take a careful bead on his quarry, assume a steady position, hold his breath, and squeeze off a shot. All of these are essential elements of precision shooting—the kind of shooting a true rifleman delights in no matter what the size of the target.

The usual rifle-shooting positions—prone, sitting, or kneeling—are difficult to assume in the squirrel woods, where most shots are at high angles. The squirrel hunter is well advised to carry the lessons learned while shooting from these positions into the woods, but to leave the positions themselves on the rifle range. Shooting offhand is worth doing on occasion at short range, but the squirrel presents such a small target that maintaining consistent accuracy in this position is just about impossible.

So when the rifleman selects a stand in the squirrel woods, he should try to place himself so that he has small tree, the branch of a larger one, or a similar solid rest between himself and the most likely spot he will see his quarry. Low branches, boulders, and improvised rests all work, but I usually prefer a

Taking an offhand shot is risky, but a roaming gray squirrel won't always give you time to set up.

small tree. A smooth, vertical rest makes it easier to move the rifle up or down to adjust for the elevation and location of the squirrel. It is easy to grip the tree or sapling firmly (with the left hand for right-handed shooters or vice versa for lefties), and then rest the rifle on that hand. This provides a steady rest and allows for accurate shooting. Leaning the body against a larger tree also steadies the shooter. Some hunters even carry forked sticks on which to rest their rifles—a support much like woodchuck hunters regularly use.

Hunting from a stand allows the rifleman to make preparations for this kind of shooting before it's time to actually pull the trigger.

If the stalking hunter is lucky, a rest such as the ones described above may be available when a shooting opportunity suddenly presents itself. But often it isn't. When the shot is a long one, the additional risk required to move a few paces forward to reach a steady rest is well worth it. Occasionally, a hunter will get lucky and drop a squirrel with a quick off-hand shot, but this is trick shooting, something the average hunter should leave to the experts. There's no harm in pausing to pat yourself on the back if you a nail a shot like that on occasion, though. We all get lucky once in a while.

Often, the best rest for steadying a rifle in the woods is the trunk of a small tree.

GUNS AND AMMUNITION

Bolt-action rifles, automatics, lever actions, repeaters—all are satisfactory squirrel pieces in .22 caliber. In recent years, the little .17-caliber rifle has also seen action in the squirrel woods, although if you already own a .22 there is certainly no reason to make a change. For years I have used a pair of bolt-action Remington rifles fitted with 4-power scopes. I have had to replace the scopes several times, but the rifles are as accurate as the day I bought them.

If you are marksman enough to consistently make head shots, solid-point bullets are fine—and very accurate. They destroy very little meat. However, the solid point does not pack enough wallop for body shots. Too many squirrels, shot in the body with solid points, make it to their dens where they die slow

This nice Abert squirrel fell to a .22 rifle in Arizona. (Bob Whitaker)

deaths. For all except the most skilled shooters, hollow points are a better choice. Because these little bullets mushroom on impact, it's a good idea to aim for the midsection, where there is little meat to be damaged. Hits in this area do not damage the back or front legs, the choice portions of squirrel meat.

The Long Rifle bullet is by far the best hunting bullet. Long or short bullets have no place in the squirrel woods.

CHOOSING SIGHTS

Most .22-caliber rifles come equipped with basic open sights. Even the best of these make for poor sighting. By moving a notched slide back and forth beneath the rear sight, some adjustment in elevation can be made, but horizontal or windage adjustments are just about impossible.

Aperture, or peep, sights are much better than open sights. They are adjustable, and in heavy cover, where there is a lot of shade, they are even quicker and easier to bring on target than the more popular scope. Peep sights are a good choice for the hunter with sharp eyes, but the older nimrod, one whose eyesight is not what it used to be, usually benefits from the magnification of telescopic sights.

For most riflemen, a scoped .22-caliber rifle makes the perfect squirrel piece. Not only does the magnification give you a better sight picture, but the cross hair or post reticle brings shooting accuracy to a fine point. If you are able to hold your rifle steady the sights will put the bullet where you want it to go (assuming you've zeroed it in on the shooting range). The scope also increases visibility during the low-light hours of early morning or late afternoon, when the chances of success are greatest.

The squirrel hunter can also use his scope to study the woods for signs of game in much the same manner that the big-game hunter uses binoculars to glass hunting territory.

The inexpensive 4-power (4X) scope is well suited for the .22 rifle. Most manufacturers have designed scopes specifically for use on the little .22. These usually work great. Some veteran squirrel hunters take it a step further, equipping their rifles with

In low-light conditions a scope is invaluable for targeting small game.

expensive scopes built for big-game rifles. They prefer the wider field of vision these scopes provide.

SIGHTING-IN

One of the biggest mistakes a novice can make is to buy a new rifle and take it into the woods without first checking the accuracy of the sights. If the sights happen to provide for precise shooting right out of the box, I can assure you that it's purely accidental. Crude, open sights are the most likely to be reasonably accurate, but if you slap a scope or peep sights on your rifle the chances are slim that they will be accurate without some fine-tuning.

You can make a rough test by bore-sighting your rifle. This is a simple process by which you line the sights up on a target and then look through the empty barrel. If both the sights and the barrel are focused on the same point, the sight adjustment is at least fair. Bore-sighting permits you to make rough adjustments that will save many rounds of ammunition when you sight-in later with live ammunition. Since bore-sighting necessitates the removal of the bolt so that you can look through the bore, this method is not always possible. (For example, you will have trouble bore-sighting a muzzleloading rifle.)

Precise sighting-in means firing at a target while making adjustments in elevation and windage until you're shooting a tight group around the bull's-eye. If the sight adjustment is not too far off, it might only take a dozen shots or so to complete the task.

Let's go through a simplified sighting-in scenario. After bore-sighting the rifle the hunter squeezes off a shot at the bull's-eye. He checks the target and finds that the bullet hit above and to the right of the bull's-eye. He now adjusts the sights, moving the elevation down a click and the windage knob a click to the left. He fires another round. This one hits dead center.

Apparently, the sights are in perfect alignment, but to make certain the hunter fires another four or five rounds. If the group is centered in the bull's-eye, he can be reasonably sure that his rifle will not fail when he lines up on a fat gray squirrel in his favorite hickory grove. Precise sight corrections rarely come this quickly, but three or four adjustments will ordinarily accomplish the job.

The distance at which the rifle is sighted in is important, too, and it will depend to some degree on the type of hunting being done. If the hunter most often uses a stand or blind few of his shots will be in excess of twenty-five yards. A rifle sighted in at that range should serve him well. On the other hand, if our hunter plans to keep on the move and stalk his game, he will get many opportunities for longer shots. A rifle sighted in at forty to fifty yards would be more appropriate for this kind of shooting.

In either case, the hunter should be familiar with the trajectory of the bullet so that he can compensate for shots beyond or inside of the range for which the sights are adjusted. Out beyond that range, the hunter may have to hold a little high to compensate for the bullet's drop, whereas inside that range he may have to hold a bit low, particularly if he is using a scope that rides high on the rifle.

The hunter should also compensate for strong crosswinds by applying some "Kentucky windage," which just means assessing the prevailing winds and then holding to the left or right of the target as needed. Such adjustments are based on the judgment of the hunter, and there is no substitute for experience. Practice on the target range always helps.

CONSISTENT ACCURACY

Breathing properly and correctly squeezing the trigger are also vital for accurate rifle shooting. Both come with practice and

Most successful rifle hunters have put in a lot of practice time at the range.

self-discipline. Once you get a squirrel in the sight picture and are ready to make the shot, you should take a deep breath, smoothly release some of it, hold your breath, and then squeeze the trigger. I repeat, *squeeze* the trigger. The rifleman who jerks the trigger as if he were shooting a shotgun will most likely pull the sights—and his bullet— off the target.

The only exception to this breathing and squeezing routine comes when you are shooting offhand. Even then, you may have time to hold your breath, but unless you are unusually steady in the offhand position, the sights will wander back and forth across the target. The only thing you can do is chance a hasty shot as the sights swing on the target—and hope.

Some hunters like to try for running squirrels, ones traveling rapidly through the trees. They attempt to get off a quick shot during the split second or two that a scampering squirrel hesitates before leaping from one tree to another. A few sharpshooters can do this successfully, but the rest of us usually need to choose our shots more carefully.

Chapter

7

SHOTGUNNING FOR SQUIRRELS

Many dedicated squirrel hunters go after their favorite game with a shotgun. I have no quarrel with them. Most are fine sportsmen and recognize the limitations of their guns. They strive for clean kills and pass up long shots—those beyond the effective range of scatterguns. No one can ask more of a hunter.

I have kind of a mental block about hunting squirrels with a shotgun, but I think it's because I do a variety of shooting. I own a number of rifles and shotguns, plus several hunting bows and a muzzleloading rifle. When I plan to go squirrel hunting I almost subconsciously reach for one of the .22-caliber rifles in my gun rack. I simply don't associate the shotgun with squirrel hunting, though I often hunt in places where only the shotgun is permitted.

To me, the shotgun is for wingshooting. It's a gun that permits me to swing on a moving target and get a string of shot out in front of it. I find it difficult to associate the shotgun with a stationary target such as a squirrel perched on its haunches eating a nut, although it can be quite effective.

Shots at stationary targets are usually child's play for shotgunners.

But the shotgun has its limitations in the squirrel woods. Beyond simple aesthetics, there are more practical considerations. The shotgun lacks the range of the .22- caliber rifle, which can be a major drawback in certain situations. A squirrel perched in the top of a tall tree may be a tempting target, but too often it is beyond the kill range of a shotgun. The squirrel has a tough hide and takes a lot of "killing" for its size, usually more than the shotgun is capable of delivering at longer ranges.

The loud bark of the shotgun also creates a problem in the squirrel woods. It shatters the serenity of the autumn setting, and spooks all of the game within several hundred yards. I can't personally recall a single instance when a shotgun blast neglected to send every squirrel in view scampering for cover.

And of course there is the minor disadvantage of hunting with a firearm that is typically much heavier than a small-caliber

But a gray squirrel racing through the trees can offer a very challenging shot.

rifle, not to mention paying for more expensive ammunition. The price tag of box of shotgun shells—twenty-five loads—is considerably above that of fifty rounds of .22-caliber ammunition.

Finally, it is practically impossible to limit the wide pattern of a shotgun to the small head of a squirrel. Invariably, the scattered pellets from a shotshell destroy more of the tasty meat.

But the shotgun has its good points, too, even in the squirrel woods. For one thing, the hunter is immediately ready for the fast-moving target sometimes presented by a spooked squirrel. It can be quite a challenge to try to nail a squirrel racing along a forest floor through brush and around trees, or to get your shot string in front of a bushytail as it swishes through the swaying tree branches, leaping from tree to tree. Shots like this will give an experienced shotgunner all he can handle, unlike an easy shot at a bushytail perched in the crotch of a tree.

Some of the finest sportsmen I know hunt squirrels with a shotgun, and they excel at bringing down a fast-disappearing squirrel—an opportunity I would have to pass on as impossible with my .22 rifle.

For a mediocre rifle shot the shotgun is probably a better bet for bringing home squirrels, if that is all the hunter is interested in. I have missed many squirrels with a rifle that would have been in the bag had I been carrying a shotgun. And certainly the shotgun may be the answer for the aging hunter with failing eyesight. With a light shotgun and a good stand near a hickory tree, old-timers can still pursue their favorite pastime.

A shotgun in the smaller gauges is also the safest firearm for youthful hunters, those just beginning their hunting careers but who still lacking mature judgment. The limited range of the shotgun makes it less risky to be in the woods with those budding nimrods, although that is no substitute for sound firearm safety practices.

One of the joys of squirrel hunting is the availability of the game. Gray squirrels often live in the lap of civilization, and the best squirrel hunting in your home territory might be just over the hill from your house. In densely populated areas the use of the rifle, even the little .22, may be illegal. In such cases, the shotgun may be the only choice available.

I ran into this situation one autumn several years ago. The Virginia Outdoor Writers Association, of which I was then president, had scheduled its annual meeting on the Marine Corps base at Quantico. In addition to workshops, we hoped to get outside to sample some of the excellent squirrel hunting for which the big military base is noted. My favorite rifle went into my old four-by-four along with my typewriter (yes, this was a few years back), cameras, and shotgun. The dove hunting was also supposed to be hot.

As it turned out, the dove hunting was spotty, but I found plenty of work for that shotgun in the squirrel woods. For the base authorities had rather foolishly used their experience with the military bullet and rifle as a basis for restricting the use of sporting rifles and soft bullets that explode or mushroom on impact with the target. Even deer hunters had to use shotguns on the base. I had trouble with that, despite the fact that I'm an old marine myself. Granted, it was back in World War II, but once a marine, always a marine.

Except for rare cases like the Quantico hunt, most of my shotgun use is limited to float trips. The boating hunter should keep in mind that the distance from his boat, which is usually situated well below the riverbanks, to the tops of shoreline trees is often beyond the range of a shotgun. He will have to pass up some challenging opportunities.

When on solid ground the shotgun hunter is probably better off stalking than waiting on a stand, for this is how most of the opportunities for moving shots develop. Squirrels are often well within shotgun range when flushed, but they rarely halt long enough for a rifle shot. The shotgunner can usually nail them on the move.

The type of cover or country being hunted generally determines how good a choice the shotgun will be. Many of the hardwood forests in the East are second-growth timber, and few of the trees tower in the sky. So the stalking hunter seldom comes upon a tree with a crown that is beyond the range of the shotgun. On the other hand, the Abert squirrel hunter in Arizona is likely to get many shooting opportunities at game in the tops of tall ponderosa pines. Such shots are usually beyond the reach of a scattergun. Few Abert hunters even consider the use of the shotgun. Besides, the Abert is a western squirrel, where the rifle is the top choice of most hunters.

Bunched squirrel tracks, with the hind prints slightly ahead of the fore prints, are a good indication that a squirrel is moving fast. The shotgun is a good choice in this situation.

A survey made in Indiana a few years ago indicated that the shotgun is a more effective squirrel piece than the rifle. According to the survey, it took Hoosier shotgunners an average of 5.3 hours of hunting time to bag a squirrel, while riflemen spent thirteen hours doing the same thing. Such surveys, however, don't address things like what methods of hunting were employed. Did the rifleman hunt from a stand or did he stalk his quarry? Did the shotgunner hunt just during the prime periods of the day? Exhaustive surveys with full information are difficult to obtain.

Another survey in Missouri showed that squirrel hunters averaged 1.22 squirrels per hour of hunting, with shotgunners again leading riflemen in the percentage of game brought down.

As I touched on earlier, the shotgun was actually my entree to the grand sport of squirrel hunting. I don't recall the exact year of this big event in my life. Nor do I remember the place or circumstances of my first squirrel kill.

I do recall that old shotgun, though—very vividly. It was a single-shot, hammer style with a thirty-inch, full-choke barrel well pitted from the use of black powder. The stock was cracked from an early hunting trip. Sometime during World War II my dad let a neighbor borrow the old Long Tom and we never saw it again. Not that I objected. It was his gun and of more value for protection than as a hunting piece. The neighborhood lad downed a squirrel, but only crippled it, and then rather foolishly proceeded to use the stock of the gun to club it to death. He was lucky that it was a single-shot gun and had not been reloaded.

This late-spring squirrel hunter enjoyed good success with his scattergun.

I was definitely over-gunned with that old blunderbuss, but it taught me a lot of lessons, and with it I picked up much valuable squirrel hunting lore. I have bought a number of shotguns since those early days, but never have I purchased one with squirrel hunting in mind.

If I were to purchase a shotgun specifically for squirrels, I believe I would select a repeater. These guns are usually lighter than automatics or doubles, and lightness is an important consideration if the hunter plans to stalk his game, as many shotgun hunters do. It takes a little longer to get off that second or third shot with a repeater, but you usually have ample time to shuck another shell into the chamber when targeting squirrels. For lightness and ease in swinging, I would stick with a 26- or 28-inch barrel and one of the lighter gauges, possibly a 16 or 20, maybe even a 28. And I would use a modified choke.

However, if you already own a shotgun or two there is no need to make the additional expenditure. Any kind of shotgun will serve you well in the squirrel woods. The shooting is not tough enough or tricky enough to demand a specialized scattergun.

Most of the squirrels that fall to my own shotgun are taken on duck-hunting trips, and my big 12-gauge waterfowl gun gets the job done, although sometimes a little better than I would prefer. Those high-brass No. 4 magnums in 12-gauge really reach out there for squirrels racing through the treetops.

No. 6 is the smallest shot size the squirrel hunter should consider, and I sometimes feel that No. 4 might be a better all-around choice. The larger size is certainly recommended if the squirrels are spooky and difficult to approach.

A lot of fine sportsmen get their kicks hunting squirrels with a shotgun.

Chapter

8

BOWS AND BLACK POWDER

BOWHUNTING

The squirrel hadn't spotted me yet, though I had been watching its busybody capers for what seemed like hours. Its approach to my stand had been painfully slow—but from the direction I had anticipated, so at least I was able to assume a shooting stance without warning my quarry. My shooting lane was clear. The range was risky, though, for so small a target.

I thought about waiting for it to move a little closer. But then I might miss my only shooting opportunity.

Suddenly I realized that my bow was at full draw, the arrow nock resting against my cheek. The busy squirrel paused momentarily, and I took quick aim at its tiny head. My fingers uncurled and the blunt-tipped arrow flashed toward the target.

The flurry of action that followed was too fast to follow completely.

The fat gray squirrel was suddenly streaking up its den tree and into a well-used hollow. Possibly my shot had been a little high, and just the brushy fletching of my arrow had tickled its back. Or maybe it jumped slightly at the twang of my bowstring.

I'll never know for sure, but my well-planned hunt had missed by a whisker.

Such is the dilemma of the bowhunter: shoot now or risk waiting. Neither alternative is foolproof.

It was late afternoon. The cold November sunset was just beginning to cast long shadows in the rich stand of Virginia hardwoods. My blind in a stand of scrub oaks offered good concealment, and the disturbance created by my brush with the squirrel had been negligible. I settled back to wait for another customer.

The squirrel is a real challenge for the bowhunter. And squirrel hunting is also an excellent way for archers to keep their skills sharp for big game. Many whitetail bowhunters have experienced the frustration of watching squirrels rustle about near their blinds, tempting them to forsake their quest for antlered game.

A bow-killed squirrel is a real prize.

The successful bowhunter relies heavily on the squirrel's habits—perhaps more so than either the rifleman or shotgunner—as the range of the bow is much more limited and the archer has to get close to his quarry.

The squirrel presents a tiny target by bowhunting standards, but it is possible for an experienced bowhunter to work within close range of the bushytail. Stalking, moving quietly, or waiting in a blind, the archer must always rely on good woodsmanship to get within effective bow range. Feeding squirrels pause at frequent intervals to look and listen—long enough for an alert archer to get a quick shot. When squirrels are abundant the shooting opportunities are many. An archer can get more shooting during a single afternoon in the squirrel woods than in a full season of deer hunting.

Shooting opportunities are varied and come from many angles—straightaway shots at squirrels that pause during a scamper up a big oak, high-angle shots at game perched in the crotch formed by a couple of tree limbs, or slanting shots at squirrels on the ground. The right-handed archer will have difficulty targeting squirrels on his right, while the lefty will probe awkwardly for game in left field. The successful squirrel

Proper shot angles are particularly important for archers.

hunter is the one who masters instinctive shooting and learns to shoot from different positions.

Many archers prefer still-hunting—moving slowly and quietly through the woods until they locate game, and then attempting to stalk within shooting range. This is an interesting and challenging form of hunting, and it's often very productive. It is recommended for woods where the hunter has not had an opportunity to scout prior to the hunt.

The method is similar to that employed by deer hunters. The bowhunter walks forward a few yards at a time, being careful to avoid twigs and dry leaves. While moving, he concentrates on minimizing noise. When he pauses, however, he studies the area carefully for signs of game. He listens for the sounds of a squirrel cutting nuts, barking at the hunter's intrusion, or scattering loose bark as it scoots up a tree. He looks for wary squirrels hugging a tree or limb, moving on the ground, or swishing from one branch to another. He hopes for a lucky break, but if the squirrel spots him first his only chance is to take advantage of what cover he can find and then wait for the squirrel to resume its feeding.

While still-hunting is a more challenging method for archers, blind hunting will put more meat in the pot. Simply locate a good feeding area or a good den tree or nest, fashion a crude blind, and wait. It is often slow hunting, but the opportunity to observe life in the woods makes the time pass quickly. A small, dull-colored campstool, the kind so popular among dove hunters, is often useful. The successful blind hunter must wait quietly for long periods, minimizing movement, and a comfortable campstool makes this easier.

Considerable thought should be given to the routes the game will most likely use when approaching the blind, and to the proper shooting positions for each. Make sure there are clear shooting lanes. The right-handed archer, for example, will want his game to approach from the front or left. The bushytail that sneaks up from the rear will be gone before the hunter can turn around. So plan accordingly.

Squirrel hunting seasons are generally long, often lasting several months. In some states squirrel hunting begins early in the summer and runs into late winter. And squirrels are sometimes included in special archery seasons.

The squirrel hunter needs a short hunting bow, something in the fifty- to fifty-five-inch class. A longer bow is cumbersome to maneuver in typical squirrel woods. Scrub brush, tree branches, and briers all hamper the archer's movements, and a small bow allows for easy handling in tight cover. The weight should be appropriate for the hunter's build and strength. There is no point in going overboard. A forty- to forty-five-pound bow is heavy enough for squirrel hunting, and a lighter one will still work just fine. Most hunters these days go afield with compound bows, but some traditionalists still use recurves or longbows. The limbs of the bow should be covered with camouflage covers or tape.

I like rubber nocking points. They facilitate the nocking of an arrow and eliminate the

While most bowhunters head afield with compound bows, recurves like this one also work well.

125

need for finger tabs. Every budding archer needs to experiment with different styles of release during practice sessions, though, as mechanical releases have also proven themselves quite accurate and easy to master. Brush buttons are advisable, and silencers soften the twang of the released bowstring. Some bowhunters these days also like bow sights.

The blunt-tipped arrows used in small-game hunting are fine for squirrels. Broadheads destroy too much of the meat and may lodge high in trees, beyond the reach of the hunter. There is

also a safety factor, the risk of injury to another hunter when an arrow is released at a high angle. In order to minimize the loss of arrows, flu-flu fletchings should be used. These are big bushy fletchings that quickly slow down the arrow after the initial burst of speed. They also drastically reduce the distance that an arrow shot from a high angle will travel when it misses. An arrow with normal fletching is easily lost in the woods.

The author scouts for sign during a bowhunt. Note the flu-flu fletchings on the arrows, which prevent them from traveling too far beyond the target.

There is no perfect quiver for squirrel hunting. A hip quiver is a fair choice, but these tend to hang up on brush or heavy vegetation. The quiver should be large enough to hold a good supply of arrows. Many bowhunters prefer the bow quiver, despite the fact that its arrow capacity is rather limited. It is definitely easier to handle in heavy cover.

An arm guard is necessary to protect the bare arm from the slap of the bowstring on warm hunting days when comfort may demand short or thin sleeves. In winter, a guard strapped to the arm holds down loose clothing. Additional tackle is mostly a matter of personal choice. At a minimum, I'd recommend bringing an extra bowstring and a knife.

Many hunters turn their noses up at squirrel hunting as too easy, but chances are they've never attempted to bag one with a bow. Bowhunting for squirrels can be an exciting sport that will test the shooting skills and woodsmanship of even the best hunters.

And best of all, squirrels have learned to live close to man and modern civilization. They are likely to be with us for many generations. So long as they are around to rustle for food, scatter nuts, and bark at intruders, the bowhunter will have a quarry worthy of his attention.

You won't usually come home with a lot of squirrels after a bowhunt, but the ones you take will mean that much more.

MUZZLELOADERS

The growth in popularity of black-powder or muzzleloader hunting in recent years has opened up exciting new challenges in squirrel hunting. The hunter armed with a front-end-loading rifle or shotgun can burn up a lot of powder in the squirrel woods. While muzzleloading hunters usually give most of their attention to deer, many are beginning to discover that small game like squirrels can also make for good hunting.

I have only one muzzleloading rifle in my gun cabinet, and it's a .50-caliber Thompson/Center carbine. Most muzzleloaders today are built with big game in mind, which means heavyweights in the .58-caliber range—too much gun for a squirrel, even the big western gray squirrel. But back in 1956, Turner Kirkland first produced his .40-caliber "squirrel rifle." And a few manufacturers have since turned out .40-caliber rifles suitable for small game.

If you can hit a target like this with an arrow or roundball, you've really done something.

Another possibility for the squirrel hunter who doesn't like being limited to a single shot is the double-barrel muzzleloading shotgun, which is usually available in 12-gauge. Or a double-barrel rifle, if one can be located.

I recently received a letter from an enthusiastic Missouri hunter who built his own muzzleloader, a .32-caliber front-end loader. The smaller calibers are out there, but they are a bit harder to locate. "Got four squirrels with it yesterday," wrote the young Missouri squirrel hunter. "I hunt for squirrels only," he noted. "They can have the rest."

Hunting squirrels with black powder or muzzleloaders is still in its infancy. But hunters using primitive weapons are always on the lookout for new game animals to pursue. And there are plenty of squirrels out there to accommodate them.

Chapter

9

THE WEATHER

As is the case in most kinds of hunting, some unforgettable squirrel hunts stand out in my memory, rising above literally hundreds of other forays into the squirrel woods. Each of these hunts was marked by some particular feature that kept it fresh in my mind. Maybe it was a big bag or a particular shot that I was proud of, possibly the unique setting of the hunt, or the evasive tactics of a particularly shrewd squirrel. But the factor that made most of those hunts interesting was the weather.

It was usually wet.

My most productive squirrel hunts have occurred when the forest floor was wet and the leaves well soaked, providing ideal stalking conditions. The sky was usually heavily overcast, a solid blanket of gray clouds that dripped a light rain—a steady drizzle that kept the woods damp and somewhat disagreeable. This is not the kind of rain that drenches you. Ordinary hunting clothes will keep you dry and comfortable for many hours in such weather. Eventually, though, dampness penetrates and the lure of an open fireplace overcomes the thrill of the hunt.

Dawn and dusk lose their significance in weather such as this. Squirrels remain active throughout the day and there is no need to arise before dawn—or to hunt after sunset. You can put in a full day, with every hour fruitful.

A half century ago, when early squirrel hunting was legal and popular in Virginia, I depended on this kind of weather to kick off a new squirrel season. Late in August the wind would shift to the northeast and gray clouds would move in, giving us several days of cool, fall-like weather, a welcome relief from the summer heat. These spells of foul weather were generally known as "three-day rains," but they were mostly light rain or drizzle, providing ideal squirrel-hunting conditions.

Such weather also boosts the hunting when it occurs later in the season, after the leaves have fallen. Some of my finest hunts have come in November or early December when a misty rain was settling down in hardwood forests stripped of their fall foliage. Stalking conditions are ideal, and the absence of foliage makes it possible for you to spot your quarry at a distance. Using larger trees for concealment, you can still get within shooting range.

That is perfect squirrel hunting weather in my book—a wet forest floor. Low hanging clouds and a drizzling rain. Midday hunting can be just as good as early dawn. On summer hunts the splash of droplets caused by a squirrel moving through the wet branches helps the hunter locate his game.

On the other hand, a heavy rain makes hunting practically impossible. Game seldom moves in such weather. Instead, bushytail is inclined to curl up in a snug, dry den and sleep it out. Such weather is miserable for both the hunter and the hunted.

Most squirrel hunting is probably done when the weather is bright and clear. It may be a hot and humid morning in late summer or a cool, crisp evening in autumn, but usually the sun is shining, making the hardwoods a delightful place to hunt. So long as the air is still and there is a minimum of wind, I like to hunt in such weather. It can certainly still be productive.

Windy days hold little appeal for either squirrels or hunters. When the wind exceeds eight or ten miles per hour the leaves and smaller tree branches are constantly moving, and squirrels, if they are out at all, take up positions on the leeward side of trees or stay on the ground. Bushytail is probably more active on windy days than it is during a heavy rain, but its activity is definitely restricted.

Windy weather also has an adverse effect on hunting conditions. During the late summer and early fall when the foliage is still heavy, the experienced hunter listens for feeding squirrels. He keeps his ears tuned for falling nut fragments that patter down through the leaves. He also watches the leafy branches for movement that gives away a squirrel's position as it travels through the forest. These squirrel signs are more difficult to detect on windy

While wet weather often produces the most squirrels for the gun, bright, sunny days make for enjoyable hunting, too.

Squirrel tracks in the snow are easy to identify and can help the hunter locate areas the animals are using.

days, when the breezes rustle loudly through the trees and keep the branches swaying.

While rain may drive squirrels to the dryness of their dens, falling snow doesn't seem to bother them—that is, unless it is accompanied by high winds and turns into a blizzard. Then all wildlife takes refuge from the storm. I have enjoyed excellent squirrel hunting when snow covered the ground. In fact, snow can give the hunter clear signs about what areas squirrels are using at any given time.

Squirrel tracks are easy to spot in winter, particularly following a fresh snowfall. And if the snow is not too deep squirrels will dig through it, apparently in search of nuts stored early in the fall for just such an emergency. Hunting squirrels when snow covers the ground is not the most productive time, but there is a unique fascination to being in the woods after a fresh snowfall. For that reason alone I often hunt squirrels under such conditions.

Squirrels, like other wildlife, are usually very active just prior to the arrival of bad weather. A winter storm front can produce some fast hunting. Get in the woods several hours before a storm is due and you may catch your quarry as it eats eagerly, storing energy in preparation for the cold, dark days ahead.

Cold weather seems to cause squirrels to vary their feeding time, but otherwise has no appreciable effect on their activities. Under normal conditions the

Hunting is sometimes especially good just before or after a snowstorm.

peak activity periods for squirrels are early and late in the day, but as the dead of winter approaches and the temperature plummets toward zero on the shortest days of the year, conventional wisdom says that bushytail is inclined to concentrate its activity around the noon hours. Still, one observer braved all weather conditions for a period of several months in temperatures ranging from 14 to 83 degrees. During this period he was unable to detect any differences in the squirrel's activity under varying degrees of heat or cold.

Deer or duck hunting often takes me into the woods or along the rivers at early hours and in extremely cold weather.

Invariably, I spot a few squirrels during bitterly cold weather—so long as it is clear and not windy.

Give consideration to local weather forecasts when planning a squirrel hunt. If there is some flexibility in your schedule, the information available at a local weather station can prove invaluable to the success of your hunt. But you shouldn't give up a planned trip solely due to the weather. As we've looked at in the preceding paragraphs, bushytail is active in most weather conditions—and the worst weather can change to the best very quickly. When it does, the hunting can be fantastic.

Some woodsmen insist that they can make long-range weather predictions based on the squirrel's appearance. One aging Georgia mountaineer observed that when the squirrel's tail is thick and shaggy in the fall, the winter will be a rough one. I don't know about that, but I do know that weather can play a role in the success or failure of your days afield. So learn to use it to your advantage.

Chapter
10

MANAGEMENT PRACTICES

Except for occasional field research and general hunting regulations, very little squirrel management has been practiced in the United States. Most states set seasons and bag limits, but the squirrel's primary needs are habitat and food, without which all management tools are useless.

CREATING AND MAINTAINING QUALITY HABITAT

The wildlife manager doesn't look for immediate results in his work, for developing good squirrel habitat from scratch may take a lifetime or two. It is never an overnight or seasonal undertaking; for once destroyed, quality habitat takes a long time to rebuild.

The task requires patience, restraint, and a willingness to work hard for future generations of squirrel hunters. The biologist who devotes his career to squirrel management will not live long enough to see and enjoy the rich harvest of much of his work. A possible exception occurs when he is able to influence the owners of a mature hardwood forest to limit their timber harvest to the extent that current squirrel populations can at least be stabilized. Rarely, however, does he have the necessary control to exercise this option.

Good quail habitat can be restored in a single growing season by planting cover and/or food patches that mature in a few short months to nourish a covey or two of birds through the winter. Rabbit habitat, too, can be had quickly by sowing wildlife patches and building brush piles for cover. To a lesser degree, wildlife clearings and improvised shelters also work for deer and other popular species of game.

But fox and gray squirrels need mature forests made up of slow-growing hardwoods, the kind of trees that offer mast and natural cavities for cover and food. While the pine and coniferous forests of the Abert and red squirrels grow more rapidly, they still require many years to mature.

Except for the occasional placing of artificial nesting boxes in woodlots devoid of natural dens, man has done little to improve the lot of the squirrel.

This little gray squirrel blends in well with the bark on the large oak behind it. Squirrels need mature hardwood forests to thrive.

A systematic approach to squirrel management would seem to require first an inventory of all present habitat in a given area. Armed with this information, the various landowners should be approached and persuaded to preserve what is left of existing habitat, recognizing that once it is destroyed replacement will literally require many decades of time and patience.

Landowners include the federal government, various state and local governments, and private parties such as farmers, estate owners, timber companies, and other corporations that hold forestlands for various reasons. Selling this diverse group of landowners on the importance of protecting our squirrel populations could well be the first major stumbling block in effective management.

In selecting forests for squirrel management, thought should be given to the species of squirrels most common to the area and to the preferred habitat for that particular species. For example, if

Den trees are vital to the squirrel's survival.

only gray squirrels are found in the area, then the emphasis should be placed on the improvement of den trees in valleys and along streams.

While nests of leaves and twigs and artificial den boxes often serve as homes for squirrels, they really need den trees to survive and prosper. Generally, the best den trees are the various oaks — white oak is probably the best — black and sour gum, cherry, hickory, tuliptree, basswood, maple, walnut, beech, sycamore, cypress, and sweet gum. Cottonwoods serve the fox squirrel in the West, and there are other variations of one kind or another scattered throughout the wide range of the squirrels.

An ideal den tree would be at least ten to fifteen inches in diameter, and the cavity in the tree would be twenty feet or more above the ground. The entrance to the den would be no larger than four inches across, as a larger opening admits moisture and predators. Many good den trees are also good mast trees. The bushytail prefers three dens: one for normal living, one as an escape den, and one in which to rear a family.

Timber managers should leave three to five den trees per acre for maximum squirrel production. The forester, contemplating the removal of what might appear to be "defective" trees, should consider the fact that it takes a den ten to twenty years to develop from the initial scar caused by falling branches or lightning.

Some trees are more susceptible to decay than others. A good den tree may develop in a beech tree within eight years, but the process in an oak may require twenty-five to thirty years. Differences in climatic conditions in various parts of the country are also an important factor. The creation of den sites usually occurs more rapidly in warm, wet climates.

While the Abert, red, and chickaree squirrels rely more heavily on nests built in the crotches of trees than do the other squirrels, good den trees still provide better homes and protection from predators and harsh weather. Red squirrels often burrow into the ground under stumps and logs.

In the absence of suitable den trees the only immediate alternative is the construction of artificial nesting boxes. These can also be used to supplement natural dens where prime trees are unevenly distributed, as is often the case. Since the boxes will sometimes be used by birds and other animals as well as squirrels, it is a good idea to install seven or eight per acre — considerably more than what is generally considered necessary for maximum squirrel protection.

Boxes constructed specifically for squirrel nests should be made of cypress or some other rot-resistant lumber. They should be ten to twelve inches wide and fourteen to sixteen inches long. The entrance hole should be two to four inches in diameter, depending on the species of squirrel most likely to use it. If only gray squirrels are present it can be small, but it should be larger for fox squirrels or western grays. In general, it should be as small as is practicable to keep predators out of the den. The hole should be located near the top of the box and close to a limb or the main trunk of the tree.

Old-fashioned nail kegs make good squirrel boxes. So do short lengths of hollow logs, and it's a simple matter to nail a roof and floor on opposite ends of the section of log.

Some biologists recommend having the bottom or floor hinged to facilitate cleaning the den every three or four years. While gray squirrels are good housekeepers, the same is not true of fox and flying squirrels and other animals or birds that might move in uninvited.

In addition to protecting den trees and installing artificial dens, good forest habitat management should include the prevention of forest fires and overgrazing by livestock and other domestic animals. Both destroy tree reproduction and damage

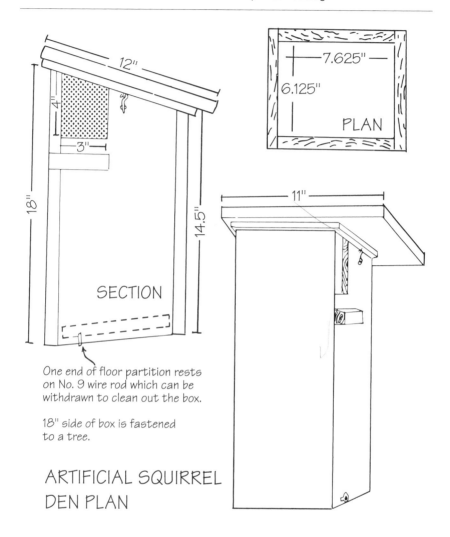

12"

7.625"

6.125"

PLAN

4"

3"

18"

14.5"

11"

SECTION

One end of floor partition rests on No. 9 wire rod which can be withdrawn to clean out the box.

18" side of box is fastened to a tree.

ARTIFICIAL SQUIRREL DEN PLAN

mature trees. Fires and livestock also wipe out vines and undergrowth, and the latter competes with squirrels for certain types of natural food.

Solid management practices for den sites and food go hand in hand. Missouri game biologist Donald Christisen notes that trees yield better nuts and fruit if they are provided enough space to develop fully. High food production is necessary for maximum squirrel populations, and it may become necessary to thin a stand of timber to provide that space in specific areas. Christisen points out that the number of feet in the crown diameter of a nut-bearing tree should be roughly twice the number of inches in the diameter of the trunk. In other words, a tree with a trunk diameter of fifteen inches should have a crown of thirty feet or so.

The best-producing timber stands include a wide variety of age groups among the trees, as this creates the most food. There should also be a number of different

Quality mast-producing trees typically have wide crowns.

species present because some trees will bear when others fail. Oaks and hickories usually form the core of a squirrel's diet, but they are not infallible. Other good producers include elm, maple, walnut, mulberry, sweet gum, ash, beech, cypress, holly, hackberry, ironwood, magnolia, pine, dogwood, cherry, wild plum, hawthorn, Osage orange, persimmon, and wild grape.

Christisen recommends an average of one elm or maple, a mulberry, and about six hickories per acre along with an even distribution of oaks. Florida biologists consider five mast-producing trees per acre to be the minimum for good squirrel habitat, and prefer a dozen such trees with trunks a minimum of ten inches in diameter. As we discussed in previous chapters, many of these

A variety of nuts sustain squirrels through the long winter months.

food-bearing trees are also prime candidates for den trees. Texas wildlife managers recommend that the so-called "weed" species such as huckleberry, persimmon, poison ivy, muscadine, post oak, magnolia, grape, rattan, hornbeam, and pecan be left in adequate numbers, too.

Food shortages can be disastrous to squirrel populations. Many migrate or die of starvation. During a severe mast shortage in Tennessee in 1968 over 90 percent of the squirrel population was lost.

While grain and bean crops can be planted to provide nourishment for squirrels, this is a stopgap solution at best. These agricultural foods don't provide sustenance for long periods of time. Such crops have been used to a limited extent for fox squirrels in Colorado, but have no widespread application.

The exact water requirement for squirrels is not known. The Abert, for example, lives in an arid climate and seems to flourish without any ready source of water. On the other hand, the gray squirrel usually lives near open water and prefers the bottom-lands and branch heads. Unless there is a permanent water sup-ply nearby, gray squirrels suffer or leave the area during periods of drought. Draining swamps also causes them to migrate. Drainage projects should be undertaken only after consideration is given to the adverse effect they will have on squirrels and other wildlife populations.

While adequate cover and food are the primary factors in the production of good squirrel habitat, other management tools are also important. Most states impose specific hunting seasons and bag limits to protect the animals during peak breeding peri-ods and to limit the possibility of exploitation.

MANAGING TO OPTIMIZE POPULATIONS

Squirrels breed twice a year, with the bulk of the annual offspring born in late winter or spring and in late summer or early fall, though there is some mating activity throughout the year. Most state game departments attempt to sandwich their squirrel sea-sons between the major fall and winter breeding periods.

A few states also open their squirrel woods for several weeks of hunting in late spring, after the year's first breeding period ends and before the second one begins. This practice seems to be slowly catching on in other states. While just a handful have gone to spring hunting so far, there is no logical reason why it can't be just as biologically sound as the fall season. Demand from sportsmen may someday make spring squirrel-hunting

Fall is usually the best time for hunters to take large bags, as annual squirrel populations are at their peak.

seasons more prevalent. Such seasons are already popular in many areas for species like black bears and turkeys.

Bushytail produces fewer offspring than many other game animals, but it seems to be more successful in rearing them. Litters range from just one to six naked little squirrels.

Exact mating time for squirrels varies among the species and according to local climatic conditions. In New Jersey the gray squirrel's mating periods are January to February and May to June, with a gestation period of approximately forty-four days. In some parts of the country, mating may begin as early as December. Delaware biologists believe that the winter breeding season produces 75 percent of the squirrels in that state. In Rhode Island the first litter is usually born in March, with a second one coming in July or August. This pattern seems to hold throughout most of the gray squirrel's range, with the first litters coming perhaps a week or two earlier in the South.

The breeding habits of the western gray vary considerably from those of the eastern variety. The western gray's breeding season runs roughly from January through July.

On average, the fox squirrel's mating period begins two weeks ahead of the gray's, although the young are still born approximately forty-four days after mating. In Mississippi the major periods in which young fox squirrels are born include late January through February and again in May or June. The peak seasons for the Mississippi gray squirrel run a little later—into March in the spring and into August in the summer.

The Abert squirrel also breeds twice a year under ideal conditions, with the gestation period averaging between forty and forty-five days.

The little red squirrel, like the Abert and gray, apparently breeds twice a year as well. The gestation period is roughly forty days after mating. The first young are born in spring or summer, usually April, May, or June.

The number of litters per year and the specific breeding periods are influenced somewhat by the condition of the squirrels' health and how well they have fed during the winter months. Females don't normally start giving birth twice a year until they are at least two years old. Yearlings and those in poor health may drop litters only once a year.

Young squirrels come out of the nest at six or seven weeks and are weaned when they reach ten to twelve weeks of age. Their life expectancy is eighteen months to six years—much greater than that of most animals. A few may even live to see fifteen years.

Males play no role in raising the young, although the more dominant animals do compete for the chance to breed females in estrus.

HUNTING REGULATIONS

Since most squirrel hunting is focused on the eastern gray, the fox, and the Abert, all of which breed twice a year, the game manager's job would seem to boil down to establishing the peak breeding periods and then setting season dates that will protect the females and the young during these critical periods.

But it's not always that simple.

In too many top squirrel-hunting states, politics play a major role. Squirrel hunting is an ancient sport, one of the oldest kinds of hunting in America. In some jurisdictions, squirrel seasons have been established by legislative acts, mostly in recognition of hunting customs instead of sound science. Such seasons may have long traditions that are deeply rooted. Often, they can only be changed by new legislative acts, and few legislators are willing to risk the wrath of squirrel hunters in their districts. As a result, it's sometimes quite difficult to bring about even badly needed changes pertaining to squirrel seasons.

Even back in colonial America late summer and early fall quickly became the most accepted squirrel-hunting times. Hickory nuts and acorns are full size by then, and squirrels occupied with cutting and harvesting nuts are easy quarry. This is also corn-harvesting time. Pioneer farmers needed an early squirrel-

Most game managers prefer a season that begins late in the year, but many states still permit early season hunts. (Pam Hallissy)

hunting season to protect their ripe crops of corn from hordes of raiding squirrels.

Game managers long ago saw the fallacy of this "early season" thinking for sustaining viable populations over the long term. The second crop of young squirrels is born during this period, and too many females are killed before the young are able to fend for themselves.

Still, these early seasons hang on in many southern and Midwestern states. As late as 1970 a bill was introduced in the General Assembly of my home state of Virginia to secure an early squirrel season in a particular county. A committee chairman, recognizing the impropriety of the General Assembly setting hunting seasons, attempted to steer the request to the Commission of Game and Inland Fisheries.

This prudent move was defeated, and Virginia gained another poorly conceived squirrel season to hamper the work of her dedicated biologists. Fortunately, in a later session a law was passed that gave the season-setting powers to what is now the Department of Game and Inland Fisheries. Virginia currently has a single squirrel season statewide.

The story of the legislator who actually lost his seat in the hallowed halls because he tampered with the squirrel season still circulates in some sections of the South. And early squirrel seasons—those that open in midsummer—often remain a point of contention. Nationally, progress is being made in the selection of the proper seasons for squirrel hunting, but the situation in a number of states indicates that political powers continue to ignore the recommendations of their own biologists.

In Missouri, a popular squirrel-hunting state, and one in which a good deal of time and effort has been devoted to the study of management techniques for both fox and gray squirrels, the season opens early in late May and continues uninterrupted well into January. While this season gives adequate protection to the first litters of the year, it seems to ignore the second crop. Such a decision evidently relies on the fact that the bulk of young squirrels are born in the spring, but serious conservationists point out the needless loss resulting from females being killed while the litters are still dependent upon them for survival.

Even though Missouri has an abundance of squirrels, the waste of a valuable resource is difficult for dedicated sportsmen to accept. A Missouri study made a few years ago showed that about half of the annual harvest is made up of juveniles and about 13 percent of the females killed are pregnant or lactating.

Georgia, Illinois, Indiana, Kansas, Kentucky, Nebraska, Ohio, Oklahoma, and Tennessee are among the states that permit mid-summer hunting, and Arkansas, California, Connecticut, Delaware, Iowa, Massachusetts, Michigan, Minnesota, New Jersey, New York, North Dakota, South Dakota, Vermont, Virginia, Wisconsin, and Wyoming open their squirrel woods in September — too early for squirrel hunting in the estimation of many biologists. Many states have moved the start of their season back to October, a month generally accepted as the safest in biological terms. Other good squirrel-hunting states should follow this example.

Most wildlife managers use bag limits to restrict the harvest of squirrels and to prevent the exploitation of the species. However, hunter checks made in most states indicate that limits accomplish little because few hunters are actually successful enough to fill them.

Illinois biologists point out that hunting has no appreciable effect on squirrel populations, as six or seven out of every ten young squirrels die within a year regardless of whether or not they are hunted. This surplus should be harvested. And doing so means hunting, a wholesome, healthy sport, as well as a way to prevent excellent food from going to waste.

Bag limits rarely play much of a role in managing squirrel populations because few hunters are able to take home a harvest like this one.

West Virginia biologists have estimated that only 13 percent of the squirrel population is taken by hunters in heavily hunted forests. A harvest of 60 percent should be permissible once the squirrel populations are stabilized.

Bag limits vary considerably. Over the years they have ranged from two per day in Florida to ten or twelve in some areas of Texas and South Carolina. Indiana has a typical limit: five per day with a possession limit of ten. Both fox and gray squirrels must be counted toward the Indiana bag limit. (Most states lump all species of game squirrels for the purpose of bag limits.) The Colorado daily and possession limits were the same as those of Indiana the last time I checked, but applied to fox squirrels only. The New York daily limit is five for all species inclusive.

In some Texas counties the possession limit is twenty, while a few counties have no bag limits and others impose weekly limits. Louisiana has a daily limit of eight and a possession limit of sixteen. My home state of Virginia for years has had a daily limit of six. A season limit of seventy-five was eliminated a few years ago as there was no way of enforcing it. Michigan has a combined limit for all species of five per day, ten in possession, and twenty-five per season. These bag limits are included only to provide a frame of reference. Changes for many of them could already be in the works. Check your local regulations before entering the squirrel woods with your favorite .22-caliber rifle.

The insignificance of bag limits is well illustrated by surveys made in a number of states in which squirrel hunting is popular. Approximately 62 percent of the licensed hunters in Louisiana hunt squirrels, and a study made several years ago revealed that the average daily bag per hunter was only two. Even at that low bag average, the annual harvest of squirrels was estimated at 1.9 million.

A similar check in West Virginia showed that only 7 percent of the squirrel hunters got their daily limit of four. A survey conducted in Missouri, a top squirrel-hunting state, revealed that the average squirrel hunter made fourteen trips afield during the long season. The average time for each trip was two hours and forty-two minutes, and the average season kill was forty-two, representing 1.14 squirrels per gun hour. During one recent Nebraska squirrel season the average harvest for the season was 6.2 bushytails per hunter.

These figures prove rather dramatically that hunters are rarely a serious threat to game populations. On the contrary, their interest in wildlife and willingness to pay for the privilege of hunting is the principal source or revenue supporting our conservation programs.

Chapter
11

TRAPPING

Trapping squirrels may be illegal in some states, but this usually has little effect on serious trappers since squirrel skins have minimal commercial value. Nor are hunters interested in trapping them when they can enjoy fair-chase hunting with .22s, or shotguns, or other weapons. The animal's bushy tail does have some value in the fishing-lure and fly-tying industries, where the tail hairs are used to dress various kinds of lures, but even this may be illegal in states where the selling of squirrel tails is prohibited.

About the only role trapping plays in the harvest of squirrels is in livetrapping them from areas where they have become a nuisance. They can then be transported to suitable habitat in nearby forests and released unharmed.

From my own accidental encounters with squirrels on the trap line, I have found that they are relatively easy to trap. They don't seem to exhibit the same degree of caution that some of the more prominent furbearers do.

Trapping is an avocation I have enjoyed since school days, when a trap line provided my brother and me with pocket money. Proceeds from trapping even gave us a step up in hunting, as they enabled us to purchase inexpensive .22-caliber rifles

Ben Hallissy uses squirrel tails to tie flies for fishing.

with which we learned to squirrel hunt. I still consider trapping one of my favorite outdoor pursuits, although I am unable to devote much time to it these days.

Several of my woodland sets have produced squirrels I would have preferred not to catch. One catch was made in a set under a boulder in a rich hardwood forest. I had placed the trap for raccoon or opossum and baited it with portions of an apple. As I was making a daily check of my trap line a few days later, the thrilling rattle of trap chains greeted me as I approached the set. I hurried expectantly forward, but was disappointed to find a mad and frightened gray squirrel firmly clamped in the jaws of the trap. I was able to depress the spring with a long stick, releasing the bushytail unhurt. It scampered off a wiser squirrel, but none the worse for the experience.

Another set that stands out vividly in my memory was one I made for mink or muskrats in a small creek. I did not bait the set, but placed it in the edge of the water beneath a little ledge, a likely place for a roving mink or muskrat to search for food. The creek flowed through a woodland meadow. A week went by without a catch, but then one morning I was elated to find the chain stretched out toward deep water. I was almost sure I had a muskrat that had drowned itself. But when I pulled the trap from the water I found a drowned squirrel in its jaws.

Most hunters have observed squirrels running along fallen trees. The little animals seem to delight in hopping on the trunk of a downed tree and racing its length. I didn't have that in mind, however, when I chopped a recess in the trunk of a fallen tree one trapping season, placed a trap in the recess, and covered it with leaves. I also scattered a few slices of apple along the trunk of the tree, hoping I could entice a raccoon or opossum to my set. The fallen tree was still sound and free of decay so I was able to fasten the trap chain to the trunk with a couple of wire staples.

That set didn't turn out as I had planned. A couple of days later I found a late-winter squirrel hanging head down in the tree and dangling a few inches from the ground—stone dead, I supposed from exposure.

So while I don't recommend the harvest of squirrels by means of a trap line, the above cases illustrate that it can certainly be done (provided you live in a state where this activity is legal). By the way, I didn't waste any of those squirrels, though I harvested them unintentionally and would have preferred not to. I used the meat on our table and shipped the tails off to a lure maker.

I'm sure that any interested hunter who is familiar with the squirrel's feeding and living habits could locate prime areas and place his traps so they would be productive. For example, a trap located at the base of a well-used den or nut tree should work just fine.

Small traps will do the job. Sizes 0 or 1 are certainly strong enough to hold a squirrel, even a big old fox squirrel. The little size 0 is probably the best choice. Walnuts or peanuts placed on the pan of the trap make good bait.

But never underestimate the ability of a trapped squirrel to deal you a serious wound. Despite their diminutive size, those sharp claws and teeth are lethal weapons. Any farm boy who has set primitive box traps for rabbits can tell you how effective the little rodent's teeth are for gnawing its way out of a rabbit trap. Box traps may catch opossum and skunks in addition to bunnies, but I don't remember ever catching a squirrel in one of my boyhood rabbit traps. However, I often saw evidence of where they chewed their way to freedom.

To my knowledge, the only serious squirrel trapping has been done by a few Canadian trappers who found a market for the pelts of red squirrels. These pelts have appeared frequently in the Canadian fur trade over the years.

Squirrel trapping in the United States is mostly limited to the activities of the various state game departments. Their biologists trap the animals alive for various purposes. Gray squirrels, in particular, often become pests when they invade parks or suburban areas and become overpopulated. As hunting isn't usually allowed in such areas, trapping becomes the main option for controlling squirrel numbers.

For livetrapping, a variety of wire or wire-lined traps can be used. (Squirrels can quickly gnaw out of wooden traps.) About the only limitation in style is the imagination of the wildlife manager who wants to study the squirrel. Such traps are baited with ears of corn, acorns, peanut butter, sunflower seeds, the aforementioned nuts, and so on.

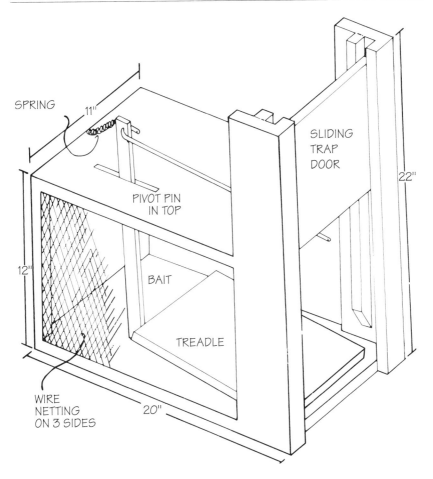

SPRING

11"

PIVOT PIN
IN TOP

SLIDING
TRAP
DOOR

22"

12"

BAIT

TREADLE

WIRE
NETTING
ON 3 SIDES

20"

WIRE-LINED TRAP FOR LIVETRAPPING

As I mentioned earlier, some eastern gray squirrel populations have somehow found their way to California and other western states—evidently after being livetrapped and released by individuals—where they thrive in city parks. This, of course, is thousands of miles west of the native range of the little critters. When their numbers must be reduced, it is almost always done by livetrapping.

They could be released in the wild in suitable habitat in the West, but wildlife biologists these days often try to avoid mixing introduced species with natives. Within their eastern range, of course, they can be released in quality habitat to boost the native population.

Livetrapping is also done for tagging purposes to aid biologists in their studies of the migratory patterns and other characteristics of the various squirrels.

Chapter
12

CLOTHING AND EQUIPMENT

The squirrel hunter should always be properly attired. By so doing he makes his time in the squirrel woods more comfortable and pleasant and enhances his chances of bagging a few bushytails. He can also improve the image of the American hunter, an image that is slightly tarnished in too many circles these days.

Let's start with a nude hunter, fresh out of bed and pajamas but eager for a dawn session with a family of squirrels in a nearby hickory grove. First, he climbs into his underwear. If the weather is warm and balmy—late summer or Indian summer—his regular short underwear will serve him well. I like boxer shorts and a white T-shirt. The boxer shorts are simple and comfortable, and the T-shirt absorbs perspiration around the armpits, protecting the outer shirt and preventing chafing.

On cool or rainy days it may be wise to discard normal underwear in favor of insulated underwear with long sleeves and legs. I prefer the close-fitting knit style. It may be the fishnet type that permits the body heat to circulate, providing warmth and dry comfort, or the double-layer thermal kind. Both types hug the body, making it possible to keep warm and comfortable without

159

adding too much bulk. With the wide range of modern synthetics now available in hunting retail stores and mail-order catalogs, there's little need for bulky long johns.

Down or quilted underwear is also good, but bulkier. Such underwear does have the advantage of a nice appearance, though, and the hunter can strip down to his quilted underwear if the weather gets too warm. He will still be smartly attired, though not well camouflaged if the garment is of a bright color.

The weather can change dramatically from early dawn to midday in most squirrel country, and the hunter should prepare for this by dressing in layers than can be peeled off as the temperature dictates.

Next come the socks. The hunter will enjoy his outing more if he keeps his feet dry and warm. The proper choice of socks will help him accomplish this. First, we have to consider the type of boots that will be worn. In warm weather, ankle-height boots will suit the squirrel hunter unless he plans to hunt in wet or marshy areas. But in cold weather or snow, ten- to twelve-inch boots are the choice of most hunters.

In warm weather, regular athletic socks are fine. For taller boots the hunter needs knee-length socks. The short ones have a tendency to work down into boots and pile up under the feet. Nothing is more uncomfortable. Socks should be all wool, though a combination of wool and nylon will wear better. Wool absorbs perspiration and helps keep the feet dry. Again, modern synthetics also possess many of the properties of wool, but with greater comfort.

Special boot socks are recommended for unusually cold weather. They are worn over regular socks as an additional layer against the cold. Sheepskin inner soles that fit into the boot are also good. Boot socks and inner soles are particularly advisable for rubber boots or those with leather tops and rubber bottoms.

In warm weather, such as one finds in most states where summer hunting is legal, I like to wear low shoes in the squirrel woods. The only exception to this is in areas where there are poisonous snakes. In these situations, boots provide added protection. Even low shoes should cover the ankles from bruises and scratches. Some hunters express a preference for canvas sneakers or tennis shoes. These are light and cool and fine for stalking, but I prefer the protection of leather for woods wear.

For most cold-weather wear, high leather boots are a good choice. They provide good protection, and if properly treated with oil or silicone, are reasonably waterproof. And many leather hunting boots now have Gore-Tex liners that remain waterproof with minimal additional care. Leather permits limited air circulation, reducing the chance of sweaty feet that will eventually get cold and clammy. However, if the going is wet and the hunter expects to wade marshy areas or to ford small streams, rubber boots are necessary. All-rubber boots are best, but at the minimum they should have rubber bottoms. Such boots are also a better choice for hunting in the snow, as some water will eventually seep through leather boots.

Insulated boots are useful in extremely cold weather, though such weather is rare in squirrel-hunting country.

Crepe rubber makes excellent soles for hunting boots and shoes. It permits the hunter to move quietly and safely through the woods without the risk of slipping on uneven terrain or loose leaves that cover a forest floor. Rubber is also good, particularly if it is cleated. Leather soles and heels are poor choices for woods wear, as they are not conducive to quiet movement and provide poor traction.

The proper care of boots and shoes is important. Leather should not be permitted to dry out, which invites rot and leakage. There are many kinds of leather conditioners on the market.

Ordinary neat's-foot oil is a longtime favorite, but there are many others. The oil should be worked into the leather, keeping it as soft and as waterproof as possible.

Camouflage outerwear should be standard attire for the squirrel hunter. In late summer or early fall green should be the predominant color in the camouflage pattern, but later in the fall and winter brown becomes less conspicuous. For summer hunting the shirt, of necessity, must be a camouflage garment, since it is usually also the outer garment. Any hunting shirt, whether summer or winter weight, should have long sleeves. In warm weather these protect the arms from sunburn and insects.

The shirt should also have a wide collar that can be turned up to protect the neck. And while most hunters wear their shirts open at the neck, they should be large enough to button up snugly when necessary. This adds warmth in winter and protection from insects in summer. Big pockets on both sides of a shirt give it a sharp appearance and provide space for carrying various items—a candy bar, ammunition, matches, compass, etc. The pockets should have button-down flaps to prevent the loss of their contents when you bend or stoop.

Brown camouflage patterns are fine once the foliage is gone, but for warm-weather hunting green shades usually work best.

For winter hunting, when a coat will be worn over the shirt, the color and pattern of the shirt becomes less important. The weight of the shirt and the warmth it will provide are the primary considerations. On warm winter days the combination of insulated underwear and a light camouflage cotton shirt is my ideal. At other times a cotton flannel shirt may be the answer. Another good combination is insulated underwear, a cotton camouflage shirt, and a reasonably heavy jacket. If the weather warms up as the sun climbs, the hunter can strip down to his shirt and still be well outfitted in camouflage clothing.

All hunting shirts should have long tails. These cover the hips and provide warmth in cold weather, and once they are tucked into hunting pants they do not work their way out like short shirttails tend to do.

Cotton pants of camouflage design worn over insulated long johns will serve well for most squirrel hunting in frigid weather. If the weather demands wool or fleece, loose camouflage hunting pants can be worn over the heavier ones.

I don't wear expensive hunting pants for most of my days in the squirrel woods, favoring instead to dress in normal street pants that come down over the tops of my boots. It should go without saying, but hunting pants should never have cuffs, as these serve no purpose and collect all kinds of debris as you walk through brush and grass.

Hunting pants should have deep, roomy pockets, and at least one of the hip pockets should have a button-down flap to hold a wallet safely. I usually carry my hunting license, permits, and other means of identification in a billfold in my left hip pocket. In the right hip pocket goes a red bandanna. I don't like a flap for this pocket because it makes the handkerchief difficult to get to.

The pants should have large belt loops so a wide belt can be worn. A narrow dress belt doesn't look good with hunting clothes, and it is not rugged enough to take the punishment an active hunter will give it. The larger belt is also much better for carrying a sheath knife, a handy item for hunting and woods use.

The choice of a hunting jacket should be given serious consideration. It must provide comfort and warmth for the hunter and a storage area for game. Trying to hunt with several squirrels in one hand and a rifle in the other can be cumbersome. When you sight game you must dispose of the squirrels before you can shoot. This consumes valuable time at a critical moment.

A regular shooting jacket with game pockets will be fine in cool weather. It should be of camouflage design, though the same effect can be achieved by wearing a light camouflage jacket over a shooting vest with game pockets. In very cold weather a wool jacket may be necessary. It can be bought with game pockets and in camouflage patterns, though a loose fitting camouflage cover can be worn over a jacket of any color—even blaze orange.

In warm weather the squirrel hunter may have to carry a small game bag slung over his shoulder. These bags are small and inconspicuous, and do not reduce the effectiveness of the hunter's camouflage clothing.

An exception to the recommendation regarding camouflage clothing must be made when the deer and squirrel seasons run concurrently or overlap. Then the need for safety overrules all other considerations. The squirrel hunter should junk his brown and green camouflage and don bright hunter orange. Camouflage patterns, however, are available in hunter orange, and these do help break up the hunter's outline. It's far from ideal, but it's a fact of the modern hunter's life.

Generally, deer seasons are short and squirrel seasons long, so an obvious solution to the blaze-orange requirement is to limit your squirrel hunting during those few weeks when the deer sea-

Squirrel hunters need to wear bright colors during deer season, although a camouflage pattern still helps.

Gloves that keep hands warm in cold weather yet allow the hunter to retain the sensitive touch of his fingers are a big asset.

son is open. Let the deer hunters have the woods then. When safety is not a factor, bright clothing should be avoided. The squirrel may be color-blind, but it can still detect sharp contrasts in color.

Summer or winter, the squirrel hunter needs a hat. In cold weather, the cap should have flaps to protect the ears. A stocking cap is warm and practical, but lacks a sun visor. Any green camouflage hat will serve for summer use. The major requirement at this time of year is a brim to shade the eyes and help conceal a bright face. A face pale from city living is one of the most conspicuous features the average hunter takes into the woods. Many hunters who rely on stalking to get their game eliminate the problem by forgoing their usual morning shave. Obviously, a full beard works even better.

For even better camouflage for the face, and to shield against annoying biting insects, you may want to consider adding a mesh head net. Bowhunters smear grease paint on their faces, a practice few squirrel hunters have adopted. It is, however, worth considering, particularly if your skin has given you away on previous hunts.

In harsh weather, you'll also need gloves to protect your hands from the cold. I prefer those with elastic wristbands that slide up under the sleeves or jacket. The glove for the shooting hand should have a slit for the trigger finger. Many hunters prefer so-called "feel gloves," wool gloves with the inside of the fingers made of silk or rayon so that the hunter retains the sensitive touch of the fingers.

For protection from sudden and unexpected rain showers a light rain suit is handy. Most are compact enough to fit into a game pocket.

Insects can be a problem during summer hunts. Mosquitoes and tiny gnats buzz incessantly, chiggers burrow into the hunter's skin and make him miserable for days, and wood ticks find flesh to which they can attach themselves. Insect repellent will keep the mosquitoes and gnats at a respectable distance, but chiggers and ticks are not as easy to repel.

The safest approach is to recognize their usual hangouts and avoid them as much as possible. Chiggers like old logs and rotting tree stumps. The woodland hunter who uses one of these for a seat during the early squirrel season is going to pay a high price in discomfort the next day. A seat on the ground with a tree as a backrest is a better choice. Not only will you avoid a bout with the chiggers, but you'll also be less conspicuous as the tree will break up your outline. Ticks are harder to avoid. They cling to grass and weeds, just waiting for a victim to pass by. While a woodland trail or old logging road may beckon the hunter, he is better off sticking to the untrod forests during tick season.

Tick repellents can be effective if used generously. Spray hunting pants thoroughly from the knees down and be sure to include the shoes and socks in this treatment. It is also a good idea to pack a small can of tick repellent on the hunt, as periodic applications

It's a good idea to spray on tick repellent before heading into woods for an early season hunt.

may be necessary, particularly if rain is likely or the grass and leaves are damp from a heavy dew.

Ticks find it easier to attach themselves to loose pants cuffs, so secure them when possible. Finally, regardless of the pains taken to avoid chiggers and ticks, remove hunting clothes as soon as possible after the hunt is completed.

Compact binoculars are handy to pack along for scanning the treetops, although riflemen can also use their scopes to clearly identify possible targets. Add a compass, a small sheath knife for the belt, sunglasses, and a waterproof box of matches for emergency purposes, and the squirrel hunter is well clothed and well outfitted—no matter whether he hunts with a shotgun, rifle, or bow and arrows.

Chapter
13

FROM THE WOODS TO THE TABLE

FIELD CARE

So, you've knocked down an elusive gray squirrel and are admiring your prize. Now what should you do?

A squirrel, like any other game animal, should be field dressed. Immediately. The process is simple. Slit the animal from the apex of its rib cavity to its tail, remove the viscera, and wipe away any excess blood. This simple procedure prevents the possibility of the meat becoming tainted.

From this point until you arrive home with your kill, protecting the meat is mostly a matter of transporting it correctly. To protect your clothing and prevent contact with other squirrels that may be in your game pocket, individual animals should be placed in a plastic bag.

A major disadvantage of the game pocket is that it limits air circulation, which is necessary to keep the meat cool and sweet. While this is of minor importance in cold weather, it can become a problem during the summer hunting season. When hunting in warm weather, use a game bag that has good air holes—such as

The hefty fox squirrel makes a nice meal if the meat is properly cared for in the field.

the angler's canvas creel with a wire bottom. Better still, use a game carrier, stringing your squirrels from your belt or transporting them slung over your shoulder.

For the ride home the game should be packed in a cool, airy place in your vehicle. Storing the kill in an ice chest works great. Run a hose from the chest so the water will drain off as the ice melts or open the plug periodically. Ideally, the squirrels should be skinned and dressed before placing them in ice, but much depends on how long the ride will be.

One of the greatest pleasures of squirrel hunting is the fine eating the little game animals can provide. If you give the meat the best of care in the field, your family will reap the rewards at dinnertime.

SKINNING

The squirrel's diet is rich in proteins, which makes its meat sweet. When properly handled, the squirrel is one of the easiest game animals to skin and clean for the pan. An expert can complete the procedure in three minutes.

Many hunters like to make a two-inch cut through the skin across the back approximately midway between the head and the tail. They work the fingers under the edge of the hide and, by pulling in opposite directions, peel the fore part forward and the hind part backward, thereby skinning the animal.

The first step in skinning is to cut through the tail close to the body. Be careful to leave the skin attached to the body, though.

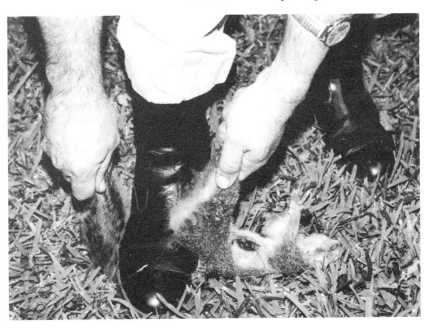

Place a foot firmly on the tail, as close to the body as possible. (Texas Parks and Wildlife)

Pull steadily upward to peel off the skin. (Texas Parks and Wildlife)

There is, however, a better method. With a sharp knife (a skinning knife is preferable) cut completely through the tailbone at the point where it joins the body, being careful not to damage the skin on the upper side of the tail. Then, with the point of the knife, slit the skin for a couple of inches along the back of the squirrel's hind legs. Now place the squirrel on the ground, belly up, and place one of your feet as close as possible to the body. Holding the tail firmly with the foot, take the squirrel by its back legs and pull gently upward.

The skin should peel off the squirrel rather easily. Work the skin down over the front legs, and then run a finger beneath the skin forward of a front leg and pull the skin all the way off the leg.

Repeat this process on the other front leg. This leaves just the head un-skinned, and if the hunter does not want to salvage the brains, he can cut the head off at the shoulders. Many people consider the brains a delicacy. If you are one of those people, by all means, skin the head too.

This skinning process leaves a small amount of skin on the belly and the back legs. Grab the skin and pull gently backward, removing it from the belly and legs. Chop off all four feet and the job is complete.

At this point, I find it easier to do a thorough cleaning by opening the squirrel all the way to its throat. Finally, wash the squirrel well in cold running water, removing all blood and foreign matter.

Before cooking or storing in the deep freeze for use later, I like to cut

Run a finger between the meat and skin of the front legs. (Texas Parks and Wildlife)

Grab the tip of skin on the squirrel's back and pull to remove the skin from the back and hind legs. (Texas Parks and Wildlife)

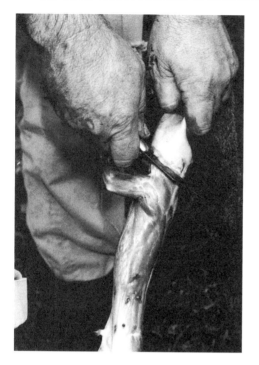

Finally, remove the head and feet. (Texas Parks and Wildlife)

the squirrel into six parts— four legs, the rib cavity, and the tenderloins.

FOOD ON THE TABLE

It has been estimated that more than twenty-five million pounds of squirrel meat is consumed in American households each year. When you consider that in Missouri alone half the harvest each year is made up of big fox squirrels running two to three pounds, this figure seems quite reasonable.

The meat of the squirrel is milder in flavor than that of many game animals and is particularly good in the fall when the principal diet consists of various kinds of nuts. The meat is light red or pink in color and makes a delicious meal.

I believe the tastiest squirrel I ever ate was placed before me fresh from a camp stove in Missouri. I had collected several grays on a morning hunt, and two of them were young of the year, probably seven or eight months old. The tenderness of those two squirrels first became evident when I noticed the ease with which I was able to skin and dress them. My wife fried them over the camp stove, and we were both amazed at the delicious meal they made—extremely tender and tasty.

With a little experience, you'll learn to distinguish old squirrels from young ones and can then tailor your recipes accordingly. The old ones are usually larger and their meat is much darker—a deep red. The young ones are easier to skin and their bones break more easily. Adult male squirrels have large, blackened scrotums and adult females have prominent nipples with dark pigmentation. The tails of young squirrels are generally more pointed at the tips than those of adults.

Young squirrels are ready for cooking as soon as they are dressed, but the meat of old ones must be tenderized by boiling—regardless of how they are eventually prepared for the table.

Now let's look at a few simple recipes that work well with squirrel meat.

After a young squirrel has been cleaned and dressed as described above, rub the pieces with salt and pepper, dredge them in flour, and place them one layer deep in a heavy skillet containing a quarter inch of shortening. Cook the pieces slowly over a medium fire, turning them until they are evenly browned. The fried squirrel is ready to eat.

If you'd like to make gravy, place a heaping tablespoon of flour in the residue and stir until it browns. Add milk and cook until the desired thickness is reached. Finally, add salt and pepper to taste.

Bob Hart, an Ozark squirrel hunter I met, likes squirrel stew with dumplings. It is a fine way to prepare an old squirrel that is likely to be tough. Well salted and peppered, the squirrel is placed in a stew pot, covered with water, and brought to a boil. It is then boiled slowly until the meat is tender.

To make the dumplings, mix flour, shortening, and salt, add water, and mix thoroughly. Place the mixture on a flour board and knead until it is about as stiff as biscuit dough. Roll it out to a thickness of a quarter inch and cut it into strips approximately half an inch wide and three inches long.

Now place four tablespoons of butter in the boiling water as seasoning, and drop the dumplings in. They should be ready in about twelve to fifteen minutes.

Brunswick stew is another favorite of squirrel hunters everywhere. To make it, salt and pepper the squirrels and place them in a stew pot with enough water to immerse them completely. Cover the pot and let the contents simmer for approximately an hour. Then add potatoes, green peppers, onions, and okra, and boil for an additional forty-five minutes. Add lima beans, corn, and butter, and cook for fifteen more minutes. Some cooks prefer tomatoes in place of okra.

A squirrel hunter's education is not complete until he has sat down to a well-prepared Brunswick stew.

For a squirrel barbecue, select a young squirrel of the year. Do not skin. Heat a gallon of water to boil and dip the squirrel in the water until the hair slips. Scrape off the hair (hog dress), clean, eviscerate, and wash clean. Salt, pepper (freshly ground), and dust with paprika.

Let the whole animal marinate overnight in the following:

3 tablespoons salad oil
2 tablespoons French dressing
¼ stick (not ¼ pound) butter
1 tablespoon salt
½ dozen peppercorns
1 small onion and celery stalk (cut up)
1 cup Burgundy wine

Remove the squirrel from the marinade and wipe dry. Save marinade. Break open the chest (rib cage) and spread the animal twelve inches above coals to which you've added a small piece of hickory. Close the grill and cook for fifteen minutes. Then baste with strained marinade, repeating this step until the meat is tender. (This recipe comes courtesy of the Missouri Conservation Commission.)

Chapter
14

A BUSHYTAIL HUNT

I ripped the sheet of paper from my printer, gathered up the loose papers on my desk, stapled them together, and filed away the rough draft of another chapter in my book on squirrel hunting.

Tired from the long session at the computer, I leaned back and relaxed as I reflected on the report that had contributed so much to that chapter. It came from Missouri, where in good years Show-Me State hunters bag almost three million bushytails each year and average a squirrel or better for every hour of hunting. The excellent report also revealed that both fox and gray squirrels could be found throughout the state. Grays are most abundant in the Ozark hill country, while the big fox squirrels like the western prairies and the rolling country to the north of the Missouri River.

My mouth watered just thinking about it.

One of the reasons I was writing a book on squirrel hunting was my lifelong interest in the sport, the spark for which was fanned many years ago on a September hunt with my father in the hills of Virginia where I still live and work as an outdoor writer, turning out books, magazine articles, and a newspaper column. My Fluvanna County home is in the foothills of the

Blue Ridge Mountains. Most squirrel hunting in the Old Dominion has long since been limited to the winter months, although biologists feel that October would be a more appropriate season.

Many hunting seasons had passed since I last crept into a good hickory grove as an autumn dawn was breaking, but memories of those earlier years were still as clear as ever.

The Missouri squirrel season is a long one. Traditionally, it opens in late May and continues through summer and fall and into winter, ending in late December. And, amazingly, the popular game animal is still underharvested.

I decided to take a fall vacation in Missouri to recapture some of the joy of those boyhood hunts and to do a little field research. The harvest section of the book, which I had just completed, showed that June and early October were the peak hunting periods. October would be the perfect month to re-create my early hunts in the Virginia woods.

Most squirrel hunters stick close to home, but a trip to new areas can provide exciting hunts for different species.

"Let's take the camping trailer," suggested my wife, Ginny, when I told her of my plans. "Camping in the Ozarks should be wonderful at that time of the year." I decided to tow it behind my four-wheel-drive Scout so I would have a hunting vehicle once we arrived.

I juggled my calendar, clearing the first week in October, and a few weeks later as the sun settled behind a green Ozark hill, we unfolded the camping trailer in a delightful KOA campground on the banks of the beautiful Current River. The 900-mile drive from Virginia had taken us two days.

"Sure we've got squirrels," said R. Winston Reed, the campground manager, as he pointed to a rich stretch of woods along the river to the north of the campground. "There's a mile and a half of timber and you can hunt all you want."

It was getting too late to hunt by the time we had our camp set up, and we were tired after the long drive from home. So we decided to drive back into Van Buren, the seat of Carter County, for dinner. I wanted to hit the woods at dawn the next day and still needed a hunting license. We had passed through town en route to the campground, and I recalled seeing a motel advertising hunting and fishing licenses. Motels tend to keep long hours, and I was hoping I wouldn't have to wait until the county clerk's office opened the next day.

"Mr. Coleman doesn't let us sell nonresident hunting licenses," said the clerk at the motel. "We don't get enough calls for them. You can get one from him, though."

"At this hour?" I looked at my watch. It was 8 PM—and Sunday.

"Mr. Coleman won't mind." She gave me directions to his home.

And affable Clarence Coleman really didn't seem to mind when a few minutes later I knocked on his door somewhat apprehensively. He assured me a license would be no problem and told me to meet him in his office several blocks away in the Carter County courthouse.

As he wrote out my license we discussed squirrel hunting. He assured me I wouldn't have any problem finding a place to hunt. Most of the private land thereabouts and the sprawling Mark Twain National Forest were open to squirrel hunting.

"You ought to get in touch with Bob Hart," he said as I handed him twenty-five dollars to cover the cost of a nonresident small-game license. "Bob has good squirrel dogs, and I'm sure he can round up some squirrels for you."

I have never been too keen on hunting squirrels with dogs, but I promised to get in touch with Mr. Hart. He gave me directions to his farm.

Before turning in that night I got my hunting gear together and put it in the Scout so I wouldn't have to fumble around in the dark the next morning. Winston Reed had suggested I drive up the river to the edge of the woods.

I slept fitfully and was awake before dawn. A heavy fog had moved into the Current River country during the night and the jungle-like vegetation along the river was dripping wet as I moved gingerly into the woods. It was still too dark for game to move, so I located a fallen tree and settled down to wait for daylight.

Dawn was painfully slow to arrive, and the fog and mist hung tenaciously along the river. It was barely light when I sighted my first game. It was just a glimpse, though—no time to get off even a snap shot. Encouraged, I leaned eagerly forward, hoping to get a fat fox or gray squirrel in the 4X scope on my .22-caliber Remington bolt-action rifle. The little .22 is my favorite squirrel-hunting weapon. I rarely use anything else.

Long minutes slipped by.

Daylight now had a foothold, and although the sun didn't stand a chance in the heavy fog, it was light enough to study the forest. The patch of woods I was hunting was narrow and flat, a small peninsula between the main river and a feeder stream that wound down from the hills. Giant sycamores dominated the stand of timber, but a good mixture of vines and smaller trees filled the spaces between them. It was not ideal squirrel cover as I knew it, but I was not as familiar with fox squirrel habitat. The big red squirrels, as Ozark hunters call them, are not found in my favorite cover back East.

Quak-quak-quak-quak-qu-a-a-a! The noisy bark of a bushytail shattered the wet morning air. I froze and—I must confess—tensed up. *Chirr-chirr!* There it was again.

Then I spotted it—directly in front of me, perched on a big vine swinging from a leaning sycamore that stretched out over the river.

Ever so slowly I raised my rifle to an offhand position. No chance now to look for a rest to steady it. I settled the cross hairs of the scope on its midriff, and then raised the point of aim slightly to compensate for the extremely short range. I squeezed the trigger. The little rifle cracked, and the squirrel flipped over backwards, clung to the vine a moment or two, and then tumbled out of sight behind the riverbank.

I had no idea what kind of water lay beyond the bank. If the current was swift my prize would disappear in a hurry. Throwing caution to the wind and at the risk of spooking any other game in the vicinity, I rushed to the riverbank.

Fortunately, the water was shallow and grassy there, and I slid down the bank to retrieve my squirrel. It took me a minute to locate it, but I finally spotted it in about two inches of water. I was delighted to see that it was a big fox squirrel, a fine way to open a

Missouri squirrel hunt. It was drenched, though, and more nearly resembled a drowned muskrat—except for its bushy tail.

Since there was little likelihood of any game moving around that stand for the next fifteen to twenty minutes, I decided to move on. This would give me an opportunity to do a little scouting as well as hunting.

When possible, I like to scout an area before hunting it. This way I can locate cuttings, dens, and other squirrel signs and concentrate my efforts accordingly.

I had moved about twenty yards when I noticed a big gray scooting from the river toward a wooded cliff that rose on the far bank of the feeder stream. Had I been armed with a shotgun, that squirrel would have presented an interesting target, but with a rifle I didn't stand a chance. I didn't even try.

Many hunters insist that the shotgun is the better squirrel gun, and for shots such as this I agree. However, the squirrel hunter gets many shooting opportunities where the game is well beyond the range of a shotgun, yet still fair game for an accurate rifleman. And I get more satisfaction from scoring with a rifle.

I worked the little peninsula out to its tip and crossed over to land on a fallen sycamore that bridged the stream. I wanted to hunt the cliff beyond. This looked like prime squirrel cover, and I decided it was the home of that gray I had seen watering at the edge of the river. All around me was a rich hardwood forest—a good mixture of giant old oaks, hickories, gum, and beeches to name a few. I selected a likely looking spot and leaned against a tall oak to watch for game. My vigil was a brief one.

A flurry of action in the crown of a small oak caught my eye. First, there was just movement of the leafy branches, but then a bushytail appeared. This was also a frisky gray, apparently headed for breakfast in the hardwoods. It scampered along a skinny limb and then poised for a leap to another tree. I tried to get it in my scope during the brief moment it needed to get set for the jump, but I was too slow.

The tree the squirrel leapt to was larger than the first, and for some reason the quick little animal elected to descend to the forest floor. About halfway down, it stopped broadside to me to study the forest. This was my chance. I settled the cross hairs, but just as I squeezed the trigger it

A tempting shot at an alert squirrel.

moved. At the crack of my rifle, it disappeared—downward.

I was sure I had scored. But when I reached the base of the tree I could find no trace of a dead squirrel, though I carefully searched within a twenty-five-foot circle around the tree.

Suddenly there was a flurry of action directly above me, and I was deluged with a downpour from the water-laden leaves. I ran out from beneath the tree in an effort to locate my elusive quarry, but caught just a glimpse of a squirrel racing through the treetops. No chance for a shot.

Apparently, I had missed clean. What appeared to be a falling squirrel had just been an alarmed one that had jumped to the ground and scurried up another tree. It most likely put the tree between us as it scampered for safety in the lush foliage.

That little episode brought back a lesson I had learned years ago in the squirrel woods near home. On a wet morning, you can listen for the sound of falling drops of water as a squirrel's movement through the trees creates an artificial shower.

It was now eight-thirty and I had promised Ginny I would be back in camp for breakfast at nine. The hour and a half of hunting hadn't produced spectacular results, but I had seen lots of game and was well satisfied with my hunting territory. I slowly descended the cliff, crossed the fallen sycamore, and worked my way back to the vehicle.

Breakfast never tasted better. We loafed for a while, sipped a second cup of coffee, and basked in the beauty of a brisk autumn morning in the Ozarks.

"Think I'll take my shotgun and hunt a little more," I mused aloud. "Maybe I can hit one of those squirrels running from the river."

I uncased my Remington Sportsman 20-gauge bird gun, stuffed some No. 6 shells in my pocket, and climbed back into the Scout. This time I knew where I was headed after I parked the car at the edge of the woods. What had been a land of strange shadows before dawn was now familiar hunting territory.

My hunt to the tip of the peninsula produced nothing, but as I was following a faint trail near the foot of the cliff, a fat gray flashed across the trail in front of me and darted up an oak about twenty yards away. He paused momentarily in his race up the tree and perched broadside to me. It was a ridiculously easy target for a shotgun—one of the reasons I prefer a rifle for squirrel hunting most of the time.

Most of the morning was gone now, too late for productive squirrel hunting on a warm, clear day. I spent the rest of my time scouting the woods and looking for signs of squirrels.

When I arrived back in camp, Winston Reed was waiting for me. "Any luck?" he asked. He seemed disappointed that I hadn't bagged more game. "Let me go with you tomorrow," he offered, and we made plans for an early morning hunt.

After lunch Ginny and I decided to go sightseeing, planning to include a visit to Bob Hart's farm on our tour. One of the local attractions we wanted to visit was the famous Big Spring, which daily pours 840 million gallons of water into the Current River. Big Spring Park is now part of the Ozark National Scenic Riverways.

The author drops a gray squirrel with his shotgun.

Bob Hart was an affable Ozark farmer, hunter, and breeder of crack coonhounds.

"We should be able to find some squirrels," said the tanned outdoorsman, who looked to be in his sixties. We made a date for Wednesday morning.

The fog was so wet and thick Tuesday morning that Winston Reed mistook it for rain and didn't bother to get up. But my time in the Ozarks was limited, so I headed out early anyway. Besides, I like a wet morning in a squirrel woods. I reworked my route of

Bob Hart, Missouri squirrel hunter and trail hound enthusiast.

the previous day, paying close attention to the good cover I had located.

"Move just inside the woods and wait," Winston had advised. And after the first hour I did just that, spotting a couple of grays at a distance and a big fox that was well within range but that never offered a target steady enough for my .22 rifle. The fox is a much slower animal than the little gray, but also more adept at taking advantage of available concealment. As this one eluded me, I made a mental note to have a session with that squirrel later in the week.

My total take that morning was two fat grays, but as we were having our usual late breakfast, Winston rolled up in his red pickup truck and dumped three more grays on the table.

"Got to leave for a campground owner's convention in Chicago," he said, "and don't have time to clean them." After he missed our appointed time, Winston had decided to go alone. When I asked if he had seen any fox squirrels, he told me he'd hunted the hill country. "The big reds are down by the river."

Ginny and I spent the rest of the day on a leisurely canoe trip down the river to Big Spring Park, where Winston arranged for one of his men to pick us up.

I took my rifle along and added another gray to my bag as the current swept us past a heavily wooded cliff. I took a lot of pride in that shot, though it was more luck than skill. An offhand shot from a moving canoe is tricky.

The drifting canoe put a tree between the fallen squirrel and me, and I momentarily lost where I'd marked it down. As a result, we had to paddle back upstream and reenact the shot so I could pinpoint my prize.

Our canoe trip spanned the midday hours, certainly not the ideal time for squirrel hunting, though the animals usually remain more active along a stream. We flushed a couple of brightly colored fox squirrels and another gray, but I didn't get a shot. Much of our trip was through the park, where hunting is prohibited.

Ginny decided to pass up the hound hunting the next day, preferring to spend the morning in camp catching up on her reading and visiting camping neighbors. While she had also passed up my early morning hunting in favor of the warmth of her sleeping bag, she'd tagged along the rest of the time—mostly to take pictures, as she doesn't hunt.

Wednesday broke clear and warm, and I reached Bob Hart's farm just as he was returning from a quick trip to Van Buren to deliver his wife to her job at the public library.

"We'll take Little Britches," he said as he loaded her into the back of his Bronco. "A couple of puppies will follow us, but it won't matter."

I climbed into the car and we headed up a winding one-lane road to the rear of the farm. We didn't ride long before one of the puppies hit a hot scent. We skidded to a halt and Little Britches rolled out to join the chase. It was a short one.

"Treed," shouted Bob as I followed him into the woods toward the baying hounds.

We found the dogs—Little Britches and a couple of pups—yelping and swarming around a small oak that apparently held our quarry. My eyes shifted skyward as I searched the tree for our quarry.

"Sometimes they roll up like a cluster of leaves," said Bob.

We backed off from the tree in an attempt to gain a better vantage point from which to study the foliage. Meanwhile, the dogs continued to bawl and whine and paw at the trunk of the tree. Little Britches even tried to climb it.

I turned my attention to the trunk and limbs because squirrels often flatten themselves against the gray bark, relying on their own gray coat to blend in. But their ears often give them away— as this one's did. I spotted it flattened against the trunk about twenty feet up.

"I see him," I called to Bob, and using a small sapling for a rest, I centered the sights on the hiding gray and brought it down.

Bob grabbed the squirrel before the dogs had a chance to tear it to bits. He did open the animal, though, and threw the entrails to the dogs. "Keeps them interested," he said.

We climbed back into the Bronco and headed deeper into the woods. Bob drove slowly as the dogs hunted the woods along both sides of the road.

Within minutes they struck scent again and ran a bushytail into the hollow stub of a dead tree. We beat on the dead tree with rocks and tried poking sticks into its many cavities. Bob, a spry man for his years, even shinnied up a small tree near the stub to study it from the top, but to no avail.

Finally, I cut a skinny pole and as Bob ran it up the hollow tree, I leveled my rifle sights on the jagged top, hoping the squirrel might pause there for a moment or two while I got off a quick shot.

Boy, was I ever wrong.

A gray blur shot out of that hollow stub like a missile from a rocket tube, dropped to the ground, and was gone before dogs or men could react. We decided it had earned its freedom and called the dogs in.

"Hunting squirrels with dogs is best after the leaves fall," said Bob as we circled slowly back toward his home. "You can see them better then, but it takes two hunters to make it worthwhile." Bob's favorite trick was to move to one side of a tree and shake a bush or yank on a vine while a partner waits on the opposite side, hoping the squirrel will reveal its position by moving away from the commotion. The lone hunter can sometimes accomplish this by throwing rocks or sticks to the opposite side of the tree.

I thanked Bob for the interesting morning and headed back to camp for lunch.

I decided to concentrate the remainder of my time on the hardwood ridge that overlooked the river.

It was 11 AM on the day of my final hunt. A little late for grays, but fox squirrels move later in the morning and I was seated on a comfortable stand with a good view of the tree that held that big fox squirrel I had seen earlier.

I was just about to call it a day when I noticed an unusual hump high on the trunk of the tree. I studied it carefully. If it was a squirrel, it was certainly a big one. My eyes ran down the hump, and I noticed that the lower end pointed outward at about a forty-five-degree angle.

"Sure looks like a squirrel," I said to myself. But the form remained motionless.

If that hump was part of the tree a little .22 bullet wouldn't do it any harm, I decided.

The form was still frozen as I took my time, steadied the cross hairs, and squeezed off a shot. The "hump" went limp and crashed down through the branches, clinging momentarily to a leafy one about thirty feet above the ground—just long enough for a flash of red fur and a brightly colored tail to sparkle in the sun.

The squirrel hit the ground with a resounding thump, and I ran quickly to retrieve it—a real beauty.

I'd opened that hunt with a big red that tumbled into the Current River, and now I could end it with a bigger one from an Ozark cliff. In between there were many fat grays. How many? Well, the Missouri possession limit is an even dozen. It seemed a good way to end an Ozark squirrel hunt.

INDEX

Index